Board Appointments

The Definitive Guide to Gaining a Non-Executive Directorship

DAVID B SCHWARZ

AUSTRALIA'S LEADING BOARD RECRUITMENT EXPERT, INTERNATIONAL BOARD RECRUITER AND CEO OF BOARD DIRECTION

Copyright © 2017 David Schwarz

All rights reserved.

ISBN: 1517674840
ISBN-13: 978-1517674847

'There are many things in life that you cannot prepare for but gaining a board appointment is not one of them. You need to dare them not to appoint you'

David Schwarz

CONTENTS

ABOUT THE BOOK AND AUTHOR	VII
1 SO YOU WANT TO BE A NON-EXECUTIVE DIRECTOR?	1
2 YOUR BOARD ASPIRATIONS	4
3 SHOULD I BEGIN WITH A NOT-FOR-PROFIT BOARD?	9
4 GOVERNANCE TRAINING	11
5 THE PERFECT BOARD CANDIDATE	15
6 YOUR BOARD PROFILE	33
7 YOUR 'BOARD-READY' CV	46
8 YOUR BOARD-READY CV TEMPLATE	49
9 YOUR 'BOARD-READY' COVERING LETTER	52
10 BOARD APPOINTMENTS	56
11 DEVELOPING PERSONAL CONNECTIONS	58
12 THE VALUE OF (GOOD) RESEARCH	71
13 BOARD ADVERTISEMENTS	75
14 THE APPLICATION ITSELF	77

15 EXECUTIVE SEARCH FIRMS	80
16 APPROACHING BOARDS DIRECTLY	88
17 THE BOARD INTERVIEW	94
18 NON-EXECUTIVE INTERVIEW QUESTIONS	101
19 HOW LONG WILL IT TAKE TO BE APPOINTED?	104
20 HOW MUCH CAN I EXPECT TO BE PAID?	107
21 YOU HAVE BEEN OFFERED A POSITION	115
22 BOARD APPOINTMENT RESOURCES	121
23 INTRODUCING THE NON-EXECUTIVE DIRECTOR PROGRAM	123
24 HOW CAN BOARD DIRECTION HELP?	131
25 FINAL THOUGHTS	142
ABOUT THE AUTHOR	144

ABOUT THE BOOK AND AUTHOR

You already know how hard it is to find Non-Executive Director opportunities and how competitive it is to be appointed to a board, right?

Non-Executive Directors (NEDs) often describe finding their first directorship as an arduous and time-consuming process. More experienced NEDs suggest finding subsequent board roles can be equally arduous. For these reasons, the biggest mistake most people make when considering a board career is not starting the process early enough and not understanding how board appointments are made.

You may not be aware, but the majority of all board appointments are made via existing personal connections i.e. people you know already - so this is where you should begin. For this reason, this book spends considerable time providing practical advice on how you can develop meaningful relationships that result in board appointments.

If not appointed to a board via a personal connection, then it is likely that it will occur in response to an advertised vacancy or through a search firm (headhunter). Many people might not know that board applications often have guidelines - written and unwritten - and even fewer take the time to understand or adhere to them. Ignoring these guidelines can negatively impact on how your application is received and your chances of successfully being appointed. Likewise, working effectively with search firms can take practice and understanding the way they work and their motivations is invaluable when trying to get them to recommend you to their clients.

Having worked as a headhunter - putting people on boards - for more than 10 years, I know how people get board roles and what matters to most recruiters. This book clearly demonstrates how you should most effectively work with executive search firms to increase your chances of being appointed to a board by them.

Beyond leveraging your personal connections, responding to adverts and working with search firms, the final common way for individuals to gain board positions is by directly approaching the organisation on whose board you would like to serve. Again, this takes a certain amount of skill to do well. Within this book, I look at how others have done this in the past and how you also can do it.

Before beginning your board journey, you should first get 'board-ready'. This includes developing a board-appropriate CV/resume and a cover letter. Both documents should clearly evidence why you should be appointed to a board. In the respective chapters I provide a board ready template and guidelines on how to write the perfect cover letter.

There are many things in life that you cannot prepare for but a board interview is not one of them. So, should you be invited for an interview, you should also be prepared for the questions they will ask you. This book contains all the most common questions search firms use in their interviews and how to respond to them.

In addition to including practical guides and templates for how to write 'board-ready' CVs/Resumes and Cover Letters, this publication also provides a list of often-asked board interview questions.

The Author: David Schwarz

Written and researched by David Schwarz - Australia's leading board recruitment professional with more than a decade of international board and executive recruitment experience. No one knows more about how to gain a board appointment or develop a board career than David. In fact, not only has he written an internationally selling 'Board Appointments' Book that takes individuals through the individual steps required to find and gain a board directorship, he has personally written 1,500 Board CVs and has been recognised as a leading executive and board CV writer. David is also a Top 10 LinkedIn user with over 22,000 LinkedIn connections and has advised thousands of clients on how to develop a board career or gain their first board directorship.

Board Direction - www.boarddirection.com.au

Finding board roles used to be a challenging and time-consuming process that historically relied upon your personal networks, newspapers, web searches, online job boards or waiting to be 'tapped on the shoulder'. Not anymore. Board Direction provides everything you need to get board appointed.

We do this in several ways but essentially what we do is equip our members with the board opportunities and skills they need to 'dare them not to appoint you'. Simple.

Board Direction is the leading board advertising and non-executive career development firm. No organisation can demonstrate the success we have had in helping people gain a board appointment. It is led by David Schwarz - Australia's leading board recruitment professional with more than a decade of international board and executive recruitment experience.

In addition to advertising the largest, most comprehensive and diverse list of board vacancies in Australia, Board Direction also offers a range of support services. We know that it is not enough to just find board vacancies, so we also provide exclusive 'board-ready' career services like 'board-ready' resume writing and board interview training as well as one of a kind board appointment courses for those interested in taking a more pro-active approach to developing a board career.

1 SO YOU WANT TO BE A NON-EXECUTIVE DIRECTOR?

Becoming a non-executive director (NED) is an increasingly common ambition. Where once the role may have been primarily of interest to retired executives, today many more people from a wide variety of fields, and often still-in executive roles, are seeking board positions.

A non-executive directorship is attractive for a range of reasons. It can be both personally and financially rewarding. It enables individuals to contribute in different ways and to several organizations at the same time. Full-time executives are also taking up one or more board positions as a part of their professional career as it broadens their relationships, contributes to the value of their 'day job' and prepares them for future board roles. Board roles can also provide new challenges to people who no longer wish, or are not available, to work as full-time executives. There are also an expanding number of 'professional directors' whose career and main source of income is made from holding several directorships. This new breed of professional often term what they do as having a 'portfolio career'.

The good news is that there is no shortage of available board positions. An Australian Business Council publication showed there were 2,141,280 actively trading businesses in Australia at June 2012. However, the release showed the vast majority (96 per cent) of Australian businesses in June 2012 were small businesses that are unlikely to have a full board.

Discounting the small businesses, there are still approximately 85,650 businesses that are likely to have a board and who might be recruiting board members. In addition to this, there are literally thousands of government entities that have committees and boards.

A recent study I conducted found that the average board size was 8 and 50% of companies recruited a board member every year. Extrapolating these statistics means that there are approximately 685,000 board members in Australia and approximately 42,000 NED roles are filled each year.

No matter where you are in your career I firmly believe that there is a board role for all professionals. Though being appointed to a board can be challenging, as the interest of others in these sorts of positions can be overwhelming.

For many would-be directors, getting the invitation to join their first board appears to be the first challenge. However, the next appointment to a board can be equally difficult and requires considerable motivation and stamina.

It can be flattering to be asked to join a board -particularly having put in a lot of effort to get it -and very tempting to say yes immediately. However, many career directors' first response to this sort of invitation is 'no'. It is 'no' because they often cannot balance the risks to their finances, reputation or careers with the time and remuneration (if any) required of them. The message they would give you is that you should take care in seeking and/or accepting a board position and make sure you do thorough due diligence on the organisation and position itself.

The first step in fulfilling that responsibility is to choose your board positions wisely and be fully informed. There are many checks that you should make before accepting an appointment and this book provides some guidance in this regard. It also considers some issues such as looking closely at the financials of the organisation, the make-up of the board (not just whether they have big names) and whether the cultural fit is appropriate for you to make a real contribution.

While there are literally thousands of organizations that need to appoint NEDs from time to time, the fact is that opportunities to take up suitable board positions (like most senior roles) come along for individuals comparatively infrequently and not necessarily at convenient moments.

It is not uncommon for your first offer of a directorship to not appear for 12mths. So, developing and being prepared for those opportunities to arise is important as is patience.

This book is the culmination of hundreds of candidate's interviews, the preparations of countless board adverts, hundreds of conversations with chairs and members of boards and thousands of conversations with potential board members. I hope the content derived from this experience propels your board career in the right trajectory.

2 YOUR BOARD ASPIRATIONS

Liking the idea of being a director is an insufficient reason to become one. The qualities and experience required of an effective director differ from those of an effective manager or executive. A Non-Executive Directorship is a role that requires a particular blend of knowledge and behavioral competencies. It is not a job for everyone.

WHAT SORT OF BOARD SHOULD I BE APPOINTED TO?

This question is one that I am asked often by aspiring and even experienced board directors. However, I think that this is often the wrong one to consider. Instead, I recommend asking yourself the question *'If I were a Chair of a company, what sort of board would I realistically appoint myself to?'* Be critical.

Having a high level of self-awareness of your individual NED qualities is important for identifying which board roles you have a good 'fit' for and which boards you can contribute to. It may be worth seeking a mentor or fellow director's input here as their 'critical friend' approach can save you much time and heartache.

For example, I counseled a client recently who had run a significantly sized family owned manufacturing business. He was convinced that he could have an effective role to play on a board of one of the major supermarkets. He may have been able to contribute but, he was not going to have the opportunity to do so because he was not going to be appointed to these boards. Why? Primarily, because he did not have the self-awareness to recognize that he was not appropriately qualified, connected or have enough experience.

The major issue here was not so much his unrealistic aspirations but rather it was his desire to be a board member but not being passionate about serving. This approach unfortunately had three further significant and negative impacts including:

1. He became disgruntled with his board search very quickly. Other people were deemed the stumbling blocks for his lack of board opportunities.

2. His reputation suffered. Others recognised that his arrogance in believing that he could, and should, sit on any board made him an unsuitable candidate.

3. His unrealistic aspirations translated to a personal reputational risk for those he met. As such, no new introductions were forthcoming despite, no doubt, that those he met could have helped him on his journey.

Let me be clear. There is nothing wrong with having big aspirations for your board career. However, you need to balance these aspirations against your experience. This will make a significant difference to the success of your journey.

WHAT NEXT?

On the assumption that you are willing to manage your expectations and aspirations then asking yourself the kind of questions below might help narrow down the sort of board that you should, at least initially, aspire to apply for. Questions to ask yourself include:

Do I need to get paid? Only considering paid board roles can be a stumbling block for many. Instead, consider whether being part of an influential board or company that you are passionate about is enough initially?

Do I have past board experience? More on this later, but if you do not have previous governance experience, put yourself in the seat of the Chair of the board who is interviewing you. What kind of board would you realistically appoint yourself to? Are you harming your reputation by asking to sit on that board?

What is my skill set? Clearly understanding what you do and how it impacts a board is key. Think critically about how valuable your skills would be at board level. Try to consider a practical example of your potential contribution.

Where do I live? If you live some distance from where the organisation operates, think about what you would add as a board member above and beyond that which a more local candidate would? By distance, I am not talking about one side of a city to the other. I am referring to the value an interstate candidate might bring beyond that of a local contact with local connections.

What are my contacts like? Are they industry based and as such deep and narrow or shallow but broad? In either case, how do they relate to the needs of the board?

What are my timings? How quickly 'must' you get your first board appointment? Are you willing to hold out for the perfect board or will something that you are passionate about but is not perfect suffice initially?

What is my motivation for being on a board? Can you demonstrate a passion for board work and not just being a board member?

How much time do I have? Board work can be demanding and can often conflict with your executive career or personal life. Can you afford at least one day out of the office a month? Are you also willing to roll up your sleeves when required? How do your family feel about you having evening meetings?

How much preparation am I willing to do to be appointed? Applying for and being appointed to a board can be even more labor-intensive than applying for an executive role. Are you prepared for the journey?

What are my potential conflicts of interest? It is likely that you will be offered a board position in an organisation related to a sector or industry that you have worked in. Think ahead to the sorts of conflicts of interest that may arise between your current interests and some future board position. What opportunities will you need to say 'no' to?

What is my approach to risk? As a board director, you are jointly and ultimately in control of, and held legally accountable for, the decisions of the organisation. So, before deciding to launch your board career, you should consider whether to undertake some form of protection (directors insurance for example) of your financial assets. Seeking professional advice on your personal circumstances can be of assistance and highly recommended.

THE RIGHT CONTEXTUAL QUALITIES FOR BOARD WORK

Beyond these practical matters, you may also want to consider whether you have the right contextual qualities for board work. Consider whether:

Do you enjoy listening? The capacity to listen while considering the wider issues from an independently perspective is important.

Would you enjoy being part of a board with different perspectives? Board work means, by definition, working cohesively with others and on some occasions agreeing to support the board's decision whilst maintaining a different view.

Are your interpersonal skills appropriate for a board setting? Can you manage the transition from a management perspective to a strategic one?

Do you enjoy disagreement? Often being part of a board requires having the courage to disagree with your peers and management while remaining positive about the direction of the organisation.

Are you comfortable asking obvious questions? Questions that illuminate the matter for everyone.

Do you require immediate results? Can you persevere in dealing with issues that may not be resolved in the short term?

Do you have a genuine desire or passion to further the aims of the organisation? This is essential.

Managing your expectations and taking a critical look at what you have to offer a board should go some way to help you decide on the sort of board that is right for you.

3 SHOULD I BEGIN WITH A NOT-FOR-PROFIT BOARD?

Landing your first, or subsequent, board position is no easy feat. Feedback from one of my members demonstrated this - she was one of 1000 who applied for a single board role! In response to this kind of competition many people find that serving on a not for profit board is a good way to begin a board career. Indeed, it is, though I never recommend joining any board, let alone a not for profit board, solely for the reason of getting on a subsequent 'better board'.

Additionally, speaking to my members, other NEDs and reviewing recent vacancies on Board Direction (www.boarddirection.com.au) it does seem that getting access to voluntary or not for profit boards is more common than getting access to paid roles in the commercial sector.

For inexperienced board members, I do recommend starting with a NFP board - but one that you are passionate about. Beyond serving on this type of board because you are passionate about what the organisation does, there are several benefits. These include:

Giving you a taste of whether you enjoy being a board member.

Contributing to your knowledge and experience to worthwhile causes.

Utilising the opportunity as a platform to show your expertise and competence to influential people on the board who might also sit on other boards.

Providing references from fellow members that are often useful when you're being considered for other positions.

Having considered the above and being still intent on pursuing a board appointment, the first thing to do to prepare yourself for the journey ahead is by preparing your unique board profile that you can use in your board CV and in subsequent conversations.

4 GOVERNANCE TRAINING

Whether you currently sit on a board, or aspire to, a robust understanding of what constitutes good governance is essential. A great way to show your commitment to good governance - and to get an advantage over your competition for board positions - is by gaining an industry accredited qualification.

Further, the majority of board candidates that I speak to have a Governance Qualification. If you don't, then you are not comprehensively 'dare(ing) them not to appoint you'.

Whilst the importance of your governance experience cannot be ignored, it is not everything. In a competitive appointment environment (it is very competitive) and when Chairs are only wanting to appoint the 'perfect' board member, having a Governance Qualification is becoming more and more a 'must have' for board candidates.

Two Options

There are two organizations providing Governance Qualifications that I advise you to consider. Both are highly regarded by Chairs & Non-Executives:

1. The Company Directors Course, presented by The Australian Institute of Company Directors
2. The Graduate Diploma of Applied Corporate Governance, presented by The Governance Institute of Australia.

Whilst the AICD's Company Directors Course is probably better known the courses provided by the Governance Institute of Australia. Their Graduate Diploma of Applied Corporate Governance is an accredited postgraduate course that arguably sets the standard for entry into a profession in governance and includes tailored public and private sector subject options.

Their courses also include a dedicated subject on Risk and Compliance, skills that are required from more and more board members, in fact, arguably these are the most important elements for any board member to grasp. Having not only the Diploma and particularly this subject to add to your CV, can go a long way in setting you apart from other applicants vying for the same position.

More Advantages to Studying with the Governance Institute

One of the reasons I particularly like The Governance Institute of Australia, and their courses, is that they are the only independent professional association with a sole focus on the practice of governance and are the only education pathway that can lead to membership of both the Governance Institute of Australia and the **International Chartered Secretaries and Administrators** (ICSA). Membership of both these organizations can be of incredible value when applying for a board role.

Six Reasons to Get a Governance Qualification

1. Adding governance training to your CV, will demonstrate your commitment to Board work.

2. It doesn't matter how long you have served on Boards, governance training is likely to teach you things you don't already know.

3. If you do have previous Non-Executive experience, governance training will likely serve to confirm (and formalise) the things you already know - if not refresh your memory!

4. Like an MBA, it might just be the difference between being appointed or receiving that apologetic email or phone call – after all when all things are equal, a board is more likely to appoint a professionally qualified candidate than someone who is not qualified.

5. The cohort you complete the course with are your peers and may provide a strong network for you. Everybody knows that the value of a strong network cannot be over-emphasized in your search for a Board role.

6. Your Governance Training will form part of your pitch to a Board as to why they should appoint you. It is certain to help you 'dare them not to appoint you'.

Still Not Convinced?

I speak to people who are trying to or have succeeded in being appointed to a board daily. Conservatively, 75% of them have completed some form of Governance Qualification. It is a 'club' that you need to be a part of if you are serious about developing a board career and contributing effectively to the governance of an organisation.

If you don't already have a relevant Governance qualification, do consider getting one as soon as possible and dare them not to appoint you.

5 THE PERFECT BOARD CANDIDATE

There are literally thousands of boards operating in a countless number of industries across Australia and each one operates within its own context and has various peculiarities unique to them. As such, it often seems difficult to decipher exactly what they might value in a new board member. This confusion is often compounded by a board's desire to have specific and targeted skills which regularly change to match the organizations current circumstances and aspirations. All of which means it is difficult to accurately pitch yourself for a board position.

After stripping away the contextual issues, in my experience, there are essentially five criteria that need to be addressed when researching, applying or interviewing for a board opportunity. They are:

An Executive Skill Set

You must understand quite specifically what you have to offer and how your primary skills or experience will contribute at board level. Being unclear about this is a killer. I recently interviewed a potential board member who, whilst well qualified and had relevant experience, could not articulate what their role on the board would be. Needless to say, he was not appointed. So, be clear about what you have to offer and ensure that you can articulate it, and your successes.

Personal Connections

Demonstrating how your 'Personal Connections' (otherwise known as 'networks' which Malcom Gladwell in his book Tipping Point helpfully reframes) can benefit the board/organisation is key. This will mean spending time thinking about who you know (individuals or organizations), how they could help and how valuable they might be in a board context. No matter what you call them, the point is that boards want the benefit of your personal connections because the introductions you provide can, amongst other things, expedite business growth and lead to new opportunities. The value of your personal connections should not be underestimated and they offer more to an organisation than you might imagine. In the end this is a key part of your unique selling point (USP) and an important reason people get appointed to boards.

Past Governance Experience

'The best way to demonstrate future success is past success' - an old adage many adhere to because it rings true. Of course, when you think about it, it is thoroughly misleading.

I have seen clients on numerous occasions make seemingly strong appointments of a 'successful' candidate only to see these individuals fail or not live up to expectation. What is the reason for this? Because they thought past success was equal to future success but they did not take into consideration the many factors which influenced that success. For example, they may not have considered the differences in: the culture of the organizations, the teams supporting them, their family life at the time, the economic environment, etc.

However, and despite many boards overemphasizing the value of past successes, it is still something that most appointment processes take comfort from. For this reason, being able to demonstrate some form of governance experience – board or committee experience – is really valuable when applying for role. In some cases, this might mean taking a 'lowly' board role on the understanding that in that next interview or personal pitch you can state clearly that you are an 'experienced board member' - the payoff will then become obvious.

Passion

Finally, one always must remember that passion is the key to being able to effectively serve on a board. Current board members are often wildly passionate about what their organisation does. Connecting on that level is essential and not being able to do so can often be the difference between an appointment or not. So, while in some cases it is not essential for you to be passionate about what the organisation does specifically (though ideally you would be) you should at very least be passionate about what you can contribute. You must also be able to articulate that passion effectively.

Cultural Fit

The Chair works hard to ensure that the board is a functioning body. Any change to the composition to the board risks upsetting that fine balance. As such, the Chair is going to be nervous about any new board appointment - particularly one that they do not know. It is therefore essential that they are comfortable with the 'cultural fit' of an individual. There are some easy ways to provide comfort in this situation - the easiest is to demonstrate that you are not a risk by evidencing commonalities - in experience, in connections and the four areas above!

To put all of this into more familiar context the five criteria that boards look for in potential board appointees are not dissimilar from what you might expect in an executive appointment.

Skills: Someone who is qualified and capable of doing the role that is asked of them.

Experience: Someone who has done the job successfully before.

Connections: Someone who knows the sector and is connected well enough to bring additional value to the business.

Passion: Someone who really wants to see the business grow because they are passionate about what they do.

Cultural Fit: Someone, who if appointed, will work effectively with the existing board.

There is of course no such thing as a perfect candidate and there are countless reasons why you might not be appointed to a board. However, understanding what the 'appointment levers' are means that you can begin to address them and thereby increase your chance of successfully being appointed to a board. Understanding these elements is of critical importance. For this reason, the rest of this chapter is going to look at each of elements in considerable detail. I will begin with: Prior Governance Experience as this is the first thing a Chair or a Board are going to look for in a successful board candidate.

1. Prior Governance or Board Experience

Determining future success at board level

While it is not necessary for board members to get along, an effective board is one that works together to make effective and well informed decisions. All Chairs want this from their current board and to continue regardless of changes in board member composition. As such, when appointing new members, they want to ensure that individuals, in addition to having the requisite skills, can contribute successfully to the outer workings of the board. So, the question is: How does a Chair determine whether a candidate will be successful on *their* board?

One way

Adhering to the old recruitment adage *'Demonstrating past success demonstrates future success'* is one such determinant. It is a phrase I regularly hear in recruitment circles. It essentially suggests that, if a candidate was successful in a similar role in the past then they are likely to be successful in a similar role in the future.

Whilst this statement feels intuitively true, on closer inspection it is not necessarily so. Deciding on this basis can ignore the cultural, physical, economic and geographical differences between an individual operating in one organisation as opposed to another. It further underplays the personal relationships so intrinsically important at board level and the diverse and unique motivations of individual members. As such, alone, I believe, it is an unreliable gauge to measure future success.

Here's the point

There is something we all suffer from called the Fundamental Attribution Error, which is that *we "instinctively want to explain the world around us in terms of people's essential attributes"* i.e. we focus and make judgments of individuals upon immediately graspable facts first. Because of this, and regardless of how much stock you personally put in the *past success/future success* statement, your past experience weighs heavily in the minds of many decision makers. So, it is therefore essential that you make it clear you have prior governance or board level experience.

I have board experience so what do I do?

Dare them not to see you! Ensure your CV promotes your board experience clearly and include evidence of success. Just because you have sat on a board does not make you a good board member – your evidence of success does. Make sure that both elements are on the front page and in bold on any document you submit. Likewise, you want to make sure this is clear in conversations/interviews you are in. Demonstrating this sort of experience/success to Chairs and Nomination Committees means that you are on your way to being considered a 'safe hire'. However, not evidencing this success/experience, regardless of your executive skills, means that there will likely be better looking candidates in the mix.

I don't have board experience what do I do?

The obvious answer is to get some. I am aware that this response might seem flippant but bear with me. If you are intent on developing a serious board portfolio or perhaps just one or two significant roles, then you need to manage your expectations. This might mean starting from the bottom – like you had to when you began your executive career.

Start by considering small, perhaps community based organizations, to serve on boards of (there are plenty out there) or target your search to organizations/stakeholders that you know intimately and who know and trust you already (a smaller group). Taking these roles won't necessarily lead to more significant boards in their own right (and this should not be your primary motivation for taking them) but the new title of 'Non-Executive Director' just might.

Before you jump into finding a small board role an alternative might be found in your past. Have you sat on an internal or executive committee before? If so, then this goes some way to alleviating the potential anxiety a Chair might have in appointing you to your first 'proper' board as these roles suggest your ability to operate in a board environment and show some governance experience. If you haven't any committee experience you should try to get some – look for opportunities within the organisation you work for or with stakeholder organizations.

So, what do I really need to know?

Potential board members are judged heavily upon their past board experience and success at board level. You must ensure that if you already have board experience and board successes that these are immediately obvious to the organisation you are applying to. If you do not have board experience, get some – committees, small Not for Profits and the like count equally at this point in your board journey. They allow you to demonstrate future success in the minds of those who might appoint you to their board in the future.

If it is easier, think about it in a regular/executive hiring context. All things being equal who, between the two following candidates, are you more likely to lean towards hiring?

The one who has done the job before

or

The one who has not?

At board level, you want to be the one who has done the 'job' before.

Whether you have done the job before or not, for help with your board application, sign up for Board Direction's Board Application Support and give yourself the best chance at being the one to **dare them not to appoint you**.

2. Executive Skills?

People ask me regularly *'What skills do most boards want in a potential board member?'*

They are:

Finance & Accounting

Audit & Risk

Legal

These top 3 should come as no surprise and generally make up the majority skills of a board's composition. However, there are plenty more skills required by boards so, if you are not a lawyer, banker or accountant do not think your board career is over - far from it. In fact, some of the best NEDs I have met do not have legal or financial backgrounds. Instead, having at the back of your mind how sought after these skills are can help you craft a convincing reason for being appointed.

Understanding the board's skills

Boards require a diverse matrix of skills but pinning down exactly what these skills are can be difficult. There are undoubtedly others but the list below is a good place to start and might help you understand where you are likely to contribute your skills at board level.

- Accounting
- Audit
- Building/Property
- Communications/PR
- Finance
- Governance
- HR
- Industry Experience
- IT/Digital
- Legal
- Management Experience
- Marketing
- OH&S
- Policy Development
- Risk
- Senior Leadership

Strategy & Planning

Understanding what executive skills are required

Key to any board application is determining what a board wants in a new Member. In most cases finding out what it is, is fairly straight forward as you will have likely been approached because of your core skills or these skills were clearly outlined in the specifications in an advert or by a recruiter.

However, in some situations the skills required can be less clear. To counter this, you need to make yourself aware of the current/future issues that the board is concerning itself with and understand what is occurring at board level.

There are several ways this can be accomplished. Obviously, if you can, speak with the Chair or the Nominations Committee first (I strongly recommend you do this prior to submitting any application). Then grasping what they want should be easy. If you do not have access to key board members or you are still unclear of the skills required by the board, then you will need to find alternative routes to get this information.

In this situation, I strongly recommend speaking to the stakeholders of the organisation to get their perspective on the strategic challenges they believe face the organisation and the ones that they also face themselves (as they are likely to be similar). Having gathered this information, you should then be able to deduce the skills required at board level to tackle their challenges.

Once you are clear on the skills required by the board the next step is to identify where the skills gaps lie. Creating a skills matrix of the board members is a good way to start. Consider the *fictitious* board matrix below. The skills that are underrepresented indicate a deficiency - so might be areas you could contribute.

SKILLS MATRIX	Accounting	Audit	Facilities	Comms/PR	Finance	Fundraising	Governance	HR	Industry Exp	IT	Legal	Management	OH&S	Policy	Risk	Snr L'ship	Strategy
Member A	■	■		■		■	■								■		■
Member B							■	■									
Member C			■									■					
Member D								■				■			■		
Member E				■													
Member F	■		■		■												
Member G								■	■					■			
Member H									■								■
Member I	■				■		■										

By undertaking the exercise above, grasping what the most sought after skills are, understanding where you can contribute and what the strategic challenges are the board/organisation is facing should form an essential part of your application process.

By taking this approach you will be able to demonstrate being an intelligent, proactive and thoughtful applicant and also be able to speak with confidence about how your skills can contribute and compliment the work of the board - all things any board would value in a new board member.

3. Personal Connections

At the most basic level personal connections are simply people you know. If you are a frequent reader of my articles, then you would have read that these connections can be divided into 'strong ties' and 'weak ties', i.e. respectively those people you see frequently and those whom you see rarely/infrequently. It's interesting to note that your strong ties are statistically less likely to land you a new job/board position and that, counter-intuitively the weak ties are more likely to.

Networks differ from personal connections only in the

approach you take to making them. *Networking* conjures up the notion of handing out business cards at cocktail parties or work events. As such they are shallow and get stale easily. Developing personal connections on the other hand suggests a less pressurized approach where you take interest in the individual and how you can help them. As such they are easier to maintain and intrinsically have more value.

Why do boards care about your personal connections?

Being well connected suggests that you are a strong candidate.

I have rarely interviewed a candidate who has a wide range of industry connections who was not also a strong candidate. The fact that they were well connected was not the reason they were a strong candidate. Instead, they were likely to be a strong candidate because they were well connected. The difference may seem minute on first reading but in an application scenario this difference is invaluable.

You see, well connected individuals form genuine and meaningful connections over time because of the way they do business. Further, they are likely to form many of these sorts of relationships because they have been successful in their career. It is this sort of individual a Chair wants on their board.

Your connections provide some comfort as to your ability to serve on their board.

One of a Chair's roles is to maintain their board's 'fragile ecosystem' - an ecosystem that is potentially in jeopardy when any new appointment is made. For this reason, providing comfort that your appointment won't adversely affect the workings of the board is critical. A good way to do this is to evidence your (relevant) personal connections (as opposed to your networks). In doing so you can show that, were you to be appointed, you would be culturally aligned with the other board members and the workings of the board.

Of course, having strong executive or non-executive industry experience can demonstrate this as well. However, if you do not have strong personal connections then you may just be deemed too much of a risk to be appointed.

In short, evidencing relevant personal connections can go a long way to provide a Chair the comfort they need to appoint you.

Your personal connections are likely to be called on during your tenure to address a wide range of strategic and operational board issues.

It is no secret that a lot of executive decision making is done based on personal recommendations or past experience. This is true at board level as well and is probably the reason most Chairs want well connected board members sitting on their boards.

Having board members connected to a wide range of individuals that the Chair might not know but trusts or values, means that the board has access to different perspectives. These differing views add value to the board in terms of competitor knowledge or thought leadership - either of which might put them ahead of their competitors or lead the board to making more informed decisions that lead to the organisation delivering their services more effectively.

Is it all about your connections?

No, it's not just about that. There have been times when I have interviewed 'professional networkers' who have a long list of 'industry connections'. On first glance, these individuals seem impressive. However, on closer inspection, these individuals can easily be separated from candidates with genuine personal connections.

Having done this, these candidates quickly fall to the bottom of the pile of those who would be appointed. So wheeling out a list of people you 'know' in an application or interview won't work unless you have a credible story about the way you interact with them and how you can leverage them in the future.

Your personal connections count

They do. However, they count only if they are genuine. If they are, then they suggest not only that you know a lot about your industry but that you are also likely to be well respected within that industry.

Further, if you are well respected then you will bring that respect with you to the board you join. These are things that any Chair wants from a board member and as such should be something you should emphasize in your board applications.

4. Cultural Fit in a Board Appointment Context

Boards operate in a *fragile ecosystem*, where effective decision-making relies on members being able to have robust discussions whilst still maintaining working relationships. Any new board appointment might be deemed an incursion as a new member risks this delicate balance. For this reason, ensuring the cultural fit of a new member to the board is of paramount importance.

In most board recruitment processes the issue of cultural fit is rarely articulated. You won't find it in a job specification or be asked directly about it in an interview; having said that, in my experience it is never far from the minds of many Chairs or Recruiters.

Invariably, this topic arises behind the scenes and carries considerable weight in the decision-making process. So, what is it and how can you demonstrate having it?

How do you demonstrate having a cultural fit?

Many consider the cultural fit question as something poorly defined and even more difficult to address adequately in an application. It is not.

There are a number of ways you can demonstrate your appropriateness for a board appointment in terms of your cultural fit.

The most obvious is linked to your current executive experience. For example, if you work in a financial institution, then sitting on the board of a similar institution would suggest being like-minded.

By demonstrating your knowledge of, or personally knowing, board members. Equally, knowing and referencing individuals you have in common with other board members provides some comfort in your appointment.

Using the vernacular of the board/industry equally provides comfort to the appointing board that you are familiar with what they do and how they do it.

Really researching and getting into the detail of what the organisation does and evidencing this research – think mystery shopping, visiting the office, buying the product and speaking to competitors.

What does a cultural misfit look like?

On the occasions I have seen a board appointment fail, it is often due, in part, to an inappropriate cultural fit. For example, it could be that a new member does not appreciate the 'slow pace' of a board or be more/less commercially orientated than other board members. Equally, a new member might not appreciate the regulatory responsibilities of a board in a particular industry or they simply might not like the other board members or their perspectives. The end result is often a board that is fragmented, has an inability to hold a 'common line' or is unable to hold to a strategic decision.

How can you tell what the culture of a board is like?

Many of the reasons for a failed appointment can be addressed by ensuring/encouraging a candidate to undertake comprehensive due diligence. Perhaps the best way to determine your fit to a board is to sit in on a board meeting. Additionally, meeting other Directors prior to joining the board is highly encouraged, as is meeting the Chair. With the exception of the latter, in my experience, this level of due diligence rarely occurs but it is really essential. I would also add to the mix speaking with the CEO and perhaps the Auditors to round out your perception of the board and the organisation.

Surely it is not such a big deal?

It is. Cultural fit lies at the heart of many a failed board application and as such, a misfit is likely to mean a short appointment. This means wasted time and a further disruption to the board resulting in lost opportunities and unnecessary expense; things that no Chair wants and will do all they can to avoid the reputational damage associated with this failure.

All the above requires a degree of research prior to putting in an application or meeting the board. However, doing this research can mean the difference between your appointment or not. Remember, **dare them not to appoint you**.

5. Passion Counts

In many ways, this seems the most obvious of the five criteria a Chair would want from a new board member. It seems a sensible move to appoint board members who are industry experts. They would obviously be able to provide industry insights that would be of great value when it comes to strategic decision making by the board. Another advantage of having people with deep industry experience on a board, is the ability of the board to then access their relationships, connections and the kind of knowledge that only someone with a 'finger on the pulse of the industry', could contribute.

However, when looking critically at the makeup of boards, you will find in many cases that, while Chairs do value the insight that comes from industry practitioners, they equally value the perspective that comes from people outside the sector. So, despite the obvious benefits of appointing this kind of board member, in my experience finding people with deep industry knowledge is not the highest priority. Instead, Chairs want to see across the entire board a DEMONSTRABLE passion for what the organization does or is trying to do.

This may sound obvious but it is worth pausing to consider what this means from an appointment perspective.

Passion, really?

The best board members I speak to are definitely capable but more than that they are passionate about what they are doing and they can demonstrate it. They know - as do Chairs - that the missing piece of the puzzle between having the skills, experience, relationships and the cultural fit to contribute to the effective governance of an organization, is passion. They know that when times get tough, board dynamics are tested, the inevitable crisis arrives or the executive job gets busy, it is going to be the passionate ones who continue to contribute. Those less passionate, quickly drop by the wayside. For this reasons, and many more, it is the passionate individuals that Chairs look to fill their board roles.

How do you demonstrate passion?

This is a critical point and where it gets tricky; it brings us back to industry experience. To demonstrate passion for a particular industry or cause will inevitably mean that you must have had some involvement with it. The challenge many will face is how to demonstrate that whilst you might be passionate about the industry (because you have worked within it) your experience is sufficiently different to the CEO's/Executive's to warrant putting you on the board.

Why do you want to sit on this board, is a question I ask in every board interview I conduct. Beyond hoping for an answer other than 'because I saw the opportunity and liked the sound of it' (you would be surprised how many say something like this) I really want to be convinced that you are passionate about the cause and serving on the board is the best way for you to contribute. Of course, it is not good enough to just say, 'because I am passionate about the cause.' If you do use this response, you should be prepared for a follow-up question such as, 'how can you demonstrate that passion?'

The best answers I have fielded have been ones that evidence some past involvement with the industry or cause. Not necessarily as an executive (though this counts) but rather by evidencing your 'extra-professional' experience. By this I mean evidencing the things you have done outside of your executive career. It could be volunteer work or charity donations, being part of industry groups or internal committees focused on particular industry specialties.

This concept is reflected in the old adage: 'Skills will get you to the door but passion will get you through it'. Clichéd perhaps but think about it. We have all worked with very capable but unmotivated people in the past. Whilst skilled, you don't want to work with them and for obvious reasons, you would never hire them for your own business. You would look instead for someone who was passionate about contributing.

There are countless ways in which you can demonstrate your passion for a cause but many don't focus on this enough when preparing for a board career, an application or interview. Board appointments are competitive processes and I can guarantee you that even if you have the skills to contribute, if you don't have a demonstrable passion to do so you will find it very difficult to convince a Chair to take the risk of appointing you. Even if appointed, I would expect your tenure on the board to be tenuous.

In summary

How then does a Chair juggle the need for new members who understand the business of the board whilst also providing diverse thinking that will benefit the board? It all comes back to demonstrable passion.

Demonstrate your passion for the industry by demonstrating some prior or current history of involvement within the industry or for the cause.

When playing the 'industry experience' card it is of utmost importance that you know how your experience differs from that of the CEO/Executive and as such is valuable in a board scenario.

Demonstrate a personal connection or an ongoing relationship with the broader industry. This might include working with similar stakeholders, charity donations, volunteer work or industry committee links.

Being able to demonstrate your passion provides the crux of any board application and should act as a guide to which boards you should target for an appointment. It can be the hardest thing for many to do but it is worth spending time considering. Without this passion, and in a competitive environment, you simply won't be able to **dare them not to see you**.

6 YOUR BOARD PROFILE

Before any board search or appointment process takes place, it is important to develop your own unique board profile. This will become your 'board business card'.

There are literally thousands of boards operating in a countless number of industries across Australia and each one operates within its own context and will have various peculiarities.

As such, it often seems difficult to decipher what exactly each board might value in a new board member, so deciding what to write in your board profile can seem confusing. This confusion is often compounded by a board's desire to find individuals with specific and targeted skills that regularly change to match the organization's current circumstances and aspirations. All of which further means it is difficult to accurately pitch yourself for a board position. So, what do you do?

One of the main things that distinguishes a poor board profile (either written or verbal) is whether or not it contains a clear message that answers the question *'Why should you be appointed to this board?'*

Per the earlier chapter, after stripping away the contextual issues, in my experience there are essentially five criteria that need to be addressed when writing your board profile. Writing your profile, and getting it right, may take some time but it is critical you do it well because this is going to be core to your pitch for board roles – whether verbal or on paper. When done properly and used tactically it will answer the key question that every board is going to ask you 'Why should we appoint you to this board? And it will help you 'dare them not to appoint you'.

Get your story straight

To effectively write your profile, it is critical that you first understand what it is that boards want and what you have to offer. However, above all, you must be able to articulate what it is that you have to offer. Therefore, it is critically important to: get your story straight – this means you need to start thinking about, and understanding what, your board profile will be used for and you should write it in the knowledge that this is also the language you can use when you introduce yourself to new connections.

So, when writing your profile, you should keep firm in your mind not just how will you respond to the reasons people get put on boards but also who will appoint you – that is, what sort of organisation you will be pitching yourself too – as these elements will require different language to be used, and for your profile to change depending on the reader and what their organisation is seeking.

Remember, there is no such thing as a static board profile.

Fundamental Attribution Error

One of the primary reasons for writing your profile and being able to articulate it naturally is so that you can reframe the way you introduce yourself. The purpose of this is so that you ensure that the people you speak with are left in no doubt that you are a potential board member. Fortunately, this is easy to do. And the

Fundamental Attribution Error is one of the key reasons.

Malcolm Gladwell writes about this in his bestselling book 'Tipping Point'. He writes that the Fundamental Attribution Error stems from the fact that people "instinctively want to explain the world around them in terms of people's essential attributes."

In other words, they do not consider the setting, culture or external influences; rather they focus on immediately graspable facts first. So, ignorant of context, people will peg you in one way or another and cannot hold differing views simultaneously.

Let's examine this. It is likely that currently people who know you are unlikely to associate you with board directorships. They probably think of you as a: father or mother; sister or brother; an executive or an industry specialist; or perhaps they define you by your extra-professional activities – like the sports or charity work you are involved with.

You see, no matter what you do, you are going to get pegged. So, it is up to you to direct people on how they peg you. And you want them to peg you as a Non-Executive Director.

Understanding the Fundamental Attribution Error – is linked closely with having a clear board message.

Before you begin

You must:
- **Reframe your aspirations:** In this context, you are not an executive, nor a friend or a colleague any more. You need to pitch your board experience.
- **Be specific:** The worst thing you can say is that you 'can do anything'. So, be clear about what you want to do and can offer – being general just won't cut it. Being general in your description makes you immediately forgettable. Instead,

include the **details** of your experience – names, organizations and evidence is important. It is the detail that is going to provide gravitas to any application and take you from an aspirational candidate to a one with tangible successes. Conversely don't worry about being too specific – you won't lose opportunities; instead you will help people understand what you offer. It is then highly likely that they will make the connections required to be able to help.
- **Know your connections:** Understand who you are connected to – remember, connectedness shows gravitas, quality and provides comfort in your board appointment.
- **Be passionate:** Existing board members will be, and you must match this enthusiasm for what they do.

Writing Your Profile Step #1

To begin with I strongly recommend that you start your written profile with the words:

'I am a ...'

Ideally you will then state your **board** experience. If this is the case, then you would write something like *I am a Non-Executive Director (or Chair or Committee Member)*.

Following this, but within the same sentence, you should also list your past **executive** titles such as CEO, Director, Accountant, Lawyer, HR Director or the like – but only use your title – not a description of what you do, as this section is about grabbing attention.

Why begin this way? Because by doing so you will, straight off the bat, tell the Chair or the appointing body that you can, and have, done the job before. It will also likely suggest board or senior leadership experience at the very least.

As an example, in my role as a search consultant, finding someone who had done the role I was looking for before was the **very first thing** I looked for when assessing applications. Those who did not state clearly that they had done the role before I immediately shuffled to the bottom of the pack. This will be the same for busy Chairs who are searching through a large number of applications. And remember, whether it be an HR director, recruiter or the Chair – each need to convince others before you are offered an appointment – so you need to make it easy for them to do so and the easiest way to do that is to tell them you have had prior board experience.

If you haven't done the role before, that is, you have not been a Non-Executive or Committee member then you want to use key phrases to promote your board level experience. Here I recommend saying something like.

I am a Board Level… CEO or Director or something similar.

If you have not even had this level experience, then perhaps you could state that you have worked for or reported into boards before.

Having started strongly you should then continue your introductory sentence with the amount of experience you have in this space. So, if you have been a Non-Executive Director for 5 years then you should state it or, if you have been both a NED and CEO (reporting into boards) for 10 years then you should state that.

Remember you should never lie or misrepresent yourself in your CV. However, you should certainly 'guild the lily' wherever possible so be bold in your statement of your board experience.

Writing Your Profile Step #2

Following a strong opening statement, you need to support it with some detail of your experience. This is where you convince people that you are not an aspiring non-executive but rather an experienced board level professional.

Here the 2nd sentence will begin with something like:

At board level I have sat on the boards of...

You will then include **just** the names of the organizations and perhaps your board titles such as Chair or Deputy Chair and / or other committee or board titles.

Once this is done you need to demonstrate that not only did you sit on the boards of these organizations but that you were also an effective board member.

This is a key area to consider. You need to think about how you can evidence what it is that you contributed to a board. You may have overseen the accounts, a particular program, an audit, a new CEO appointment or something similar. You may also have seen the organisation grow during your tenure or had a particularly successful outcome or involvement with board matters. Spend some time and think about what it is that you contributed or can contribute to a board.

This is by far and away the most difficult thing to do. Most are afraid to reference their own success at board level as they consider themselves part of a group of individuals who make decisions. Indeed, this is true but it is also true to say that each board director makes their own contribution. You need to be clear about what this is.

Once you are clear you might want to begin with something like.

Here, I can evidence having ... (and include your successes or contribution).

Remember, this is an exercise in succinct writing so you cannot include everything – just include your greatest successes or the things you are most proud of. You don't need to do much to demonstrate that you a capable board member – just a few highlights here will do.

Writing Your Profile Step #3

The previous section may take a little time to complete but it is worth doing well as it is the most important thing for you to get right.

Once you have you should start on your executive experience. This is in response to the 2nd criteria that you will be judged against – your executive success.

This section should be easier to do than the previous section as most of it is, I hope, already in your executive CV and will come to mind fairly easily.

Here I recommend beginning with:

In an executive capacity, I am currently ... (and then enter the title and organisation that you currently work for).

Following this, briefly state your previous experience. Remember, you are trying to impress and make it readable so focus on the highest profile roles you have held in the past or the highest profile organizations you have worked for. Not everything you have ever done needs to be included here as this will be in the body of the CV (we will get to that later).

Writing Your Profile Step #4

Once done it is time to get into the detail of your executive skills. This section of your profile further addresses the specific skills you can provide but is also an opportunity for you to demonstrate

- Your Connectedness – and therefore your cultural fit
- Your passion for / and experience in the sector or industry that the board operates in.

Again, this should be fairly easy for you to do. This section will incorporate the skills that keep you employed on a day to day basis. For example, perhaps you are a commercial Lawyer, an accountant, a project manager, a manufacturing specialist or an industry expert. Whatever it is, include it here – but briefly, your CV will do the rest.

Here I recommend beginning by using words like:

Further, I can demonstrate ...

Whilst easier to do than other sections. There are some pitfalls. Remember that, despite this being about your executive experience, you are still pitching yourself for a board appointment. This means staying away from your operational experience and focusing on your strategic experience and success.

As such, do not mention the number of people you manage or how you can balance the books. Instead talk about your work with boards or the strategic guidance you have provided in the past. Equally, be specific, use names and details or figures as much as you can.

Writing Your Profile Step #5

I have already outlined why a governance qualification is important. If you have one, this is the place to show it off in addition to your other qualifications and memberships. These will all be considered as part of your application.

Remember boards want intelligent and educated people so you should try to demonstrate this. If you have an MBA include it here. If you have a degree, include it here. Likewise, if you have completed some other form of governance training, include it here.

You should also list the names of the industry or governance bodies you are a member of. These count and demonstrate intent.

Here I recommend you use the following words to begin your final sentence of your profile:
Finally, I have a ... and I am a member of...

If you don't have particularly good qualifications, then I do not recommend including them. Instead join an industry membership body such as the AICD or Governance Institute of Australia. By doing so you can then list them here and it will present you in a stronger light than having nothing at all.

A poor example

Hopefully you now you have a strong idea of how to write your board profile. But, don't rush the process of writing it as it really is important to get right.

Before I pull it all together for you in a template - let me show you a very common but very poor example of a board profile. It will go something like this.

I am seeking a board position. I have strategic experience across a number of sectors and industries. I have worked with boards before and have over 20 years' experience.

I am sure you can see what is wrong with this already but let me make it clear
- It begins with an aspirational statement – so, the assumption will be that they have not done the role before
- It is generic – therefore forgettable. If you have any generic statements in your profile you should remove them immediately. Only include what you can demonstrate success in.
- There is no detail of what they do – so they cannot evidence that they are good at it despite saying that board experience.
- There are no qualifications included – so it is assumed that they will not be intelligent or educated.

All in all, it is a fairly uninspiring, dispassionate and a forgettable introduction.

A good example

Here is a format or a template that you might want to use but feel free to make my guide your own – it is after all your document and must reflect your style. Let's go over it together. It begins with:

*I am a **BOARD TITLE** (Non-Executive, Committee Member, Chair and Director) and **EXECUTIVE TITLE** with over **NO. OF YEARS** board level experience across the **X, Y & Z** (public, private, not for profit) sectors. Specifically, I can evidence success in the following industries: **U, V & W**. At board level, some highlights include: **S, T & U**. Further, in an executive capacity I am currently the **TITLE** of **M** and was previously the **TITLE** of **O**. My primary responsibility was **J, K & L**. Finally, I have a **QUALIFICATION** and a **QUALIFICATION**. I am also a Member of the **ORGANISATION** and **ORGANISATION**.*

Your own profile is likely to be longer than this as it will include more detail and that is fine. However, if it is any more than twice as long you should consider removing some text as your success and 'board appropriateness' will be lost within if there is too much to read.

Using your Board Profile

Writing your board profile is the first step in being able to answer the question 'why should we appoint you?' Any written application is essentially asking you to answer this question. It should also feature prominently on your Board CV.

However, most of the time you will not write an application but be asked to demonstrate it verbally – through interviews but also in informal conversations with people who might have opportunities that you are not even aware of. Because of this, you will need to adapt the way you use what you have written to make it fit for purpose.

One useful way to adapt this in verbal form is by following a simple guide that incorporates just two phrases.

- *You know how…*

and

- *What I do is…*
Let me explain.

When you meet someone for the first time or someone you do not see regularly they are highly likely to ask you what you do. When this happens, you might consider responding by using words to the effect of:

You know how hard it is for boards to find directors with good legal or financial skills. *(Replace legal or financial with your unique skill).*

Well, as a non-executive director, **what I do is** *help boards assess their risks. (Or whatever it is you offer a board).*

This is a great way to begin an introduction. It takes some getting used to but it immediately works to frame how people see you and what you can offer.

Further it is also a self-selecting introduction and promotes the obvious follow up question: *'How do you do that?'*

To further explain, by starting with *'You know how'* immediately drives a positive or negative response from whoever you are speaking with.

If the response is negative – that is, they don't know how difficult it is to find good board directors then you quickly find out and can move on to other areas of discussion.

OR

If their response is positive and they do understand how difficult it is to find good board directors – then you have their attention and they will likely to want to know more.

Try it out. It is refreshingly easy to do once you get the hang of it.

I trust you will now have the bones of a strong board profile and are primed to be able to articulate it naturally. So, what next? Well, you should start by asking yourself:

Who knows that you are looking for a NED role?

If the answer is 'very few people' or 'no one' then perhaps the best thing you can do is to start telling people.

As you know most board appointments occur through personal connections. Because this is the case it is important that you let people know that you are 'board ready' and looking for a board role.

So, my **strong** recommendation is that once you are clear on what your board profile is, that you reach out to those you know already or perhaps those that are already NEDs and let them know that you are 'building a portfolio career', 'that board opportunities interest you' or something similar.

It is critically important that you begin testing out your new profile — you will be surprised how many opportunities occur by reframing your pitch or introduction and simply telling people about your board aspirations.

In fact, a client of mine recently took this advice and called me just one month after beginning to reframe her pitch. She told me that she was stunned about how effective it was and the feedback from her connections was, and I quote *'why didn't you tell'*.

7 YOUR 'BOARD-READY' CV

Whilst not all board appointments require a dedicated 'board-ready' CV, it is important to have one should one be requested from you. Furthermore, the process of writing this document can be invaluable in getting your message right and the content can be used in any future interviews.

In a recent study (http://flowingdata.com/2012/04/11/how-recruiters-look-at-your-resume/), eye tracking technology showed that decision-makers spent as little as six seconds on their initial "fit/no fit" decision when viewing CVs. With this in mind, it is essential to effectively prioritize information and to not clutter your CV or have poor formatting.

The results of the study also revealed that decision-makers could easily find and focus on the important information if they were looking at a professional CV much faster than regular resumes or an online profile. So, using a professional template where your skills, experience and attributes are clearly visible will positively affect the way your application is received.

Finally, the study found that recruiters tended to focus on pictures for the simple reason that pictures naturally draw the eye. Thus, it found that pictures often hampered recruiters from locating the most relevant information, like skills and experience.

GETTING 'BOARD-READY'

A standard 'board-ready' CV is often between one and three pages long. While there is no set template for what style or format your CV should be in, it must answer the central questions any Chair or appointing organizations will want to know which are 'Why should we appoint you?' and 'What value can you offer the board?' The information and the template below will help guide you in writing or amending your CV so it answers these questions.

Style and Font: Ensure that the formatting of your CV is standardized across the document. This includes using a basic style 11pt font as a minimum. Recent studies have found that Helvetica is the 'best' font to use.

Name: Your name should be in full and upfront and in larger font (minimum 18pt).

Contact Details: Include your contact details at the top or put them at the bottom of your CV. Ensure that they are clear and up-to-date.

Social Media: You may want to include links to your digital profile. If you do, ensure that your CV and digital profile are complementary.

Photo *(Optional)*: You may want to include a photo. It should be clear and include only your head and shoulders. When printed, it should be clear in both color and black and white. However, be aware that when including a photo, positive or negative reader biases may occur. These can be further emphasized if the photo does not print well. I don't recommend using one – besides LinkedIn will be checked if they want to know what you look like.

Non-Executive Profile: You may write in the first person and should aim not to exceed five lines. Your profile should outline the success and 'value add' your contributions as a non-executive have made. It should not include aspirational statements or ones that cannot be supported without evidence. If you have limited or no non-executive experience, focus on how your executive experience relates to the board or the strategic running of the business.

Non-Executive Success: List between two and five items demonstrating your success at board level. Again, should you not have specific non-executive experience, include your success working with or for boards.

Board/Committee Experience: List your key roles and responsibilities in reverse chronological order. Include any committees or subsidiary board experience you have had. Again, should you not have specific non-executive experience, include your success working with or for boards.

Executive Experience: List your executive experience in reverse chronological order. Include examples of working with or reporting to boards and key achievements.

Qualifications and Professional Development: In reverse chronological order, list your most relevant educational history.

Extra-Professional Activities & Memberships: List any activities or personal interests relevant to your application that cannot be incorporated in the sections above, e.g. languages, awards, charity work or personal successes.

Referees: Include the most relevant referees on your CV. Do not include their contact details.

The following chapter presents a template for a 'board-ready' CV. You may wish to use this approach in totality or use elements of it to craft your own CV.

8 YOUR BOARD-READY CV TEMPLATE

FirstName LastName

M: (Mobile)   E: (Email)   LI: (LinkedIn Address – in/…)
A: (Address)

Board Profile

This section briefly summarizes your board or committee experience (either as an executive or non-executive), how long you have been working with/in boards. Include examples of success (statistics are best), the companies and sectors you have worked with and the scope and scale of your experience. Do not include aspiration statements. Add any relevant qualifications.

Board & Executive Successes

This section briefly summarizes your board or executive successes. By nature, it will duplicate some of your experience below. However, these are the elements of your career that will demonstrate that you are and have been effective at a very senior level. As with the entire CV this section should focus on quantifiable/demonstrable success.

Non-Executive & Committee Experience

This section lists, in descending order from most recent, your board or committee experience. Do not limit your examples with just formal board roles you can legitimately include sub-committee or committee memberships and other roles that had a strategic or governance perspective. When providing evidence of success, please again be specific and try not to make statements that you cannot support with evidence – for example: Stating that you were a board member does not demonstrate that you were a good board member!

Executive Board Experience

This section lists, again in descending order, your executive board career roles.

Executive Experience

This section lists, again in descending order, your executive career roles. Again, please be as specific as possible when listing your successes and include statistics or numerical evidence. For example, just stating that you were a senior executive does not demonstrate that you were good senior executive!

Qualifications & Professional development

This section lists, again in descending order, your qualifications and education as well as any relevant professional development

Extra-Professional Experience & Interests

This section lists your professional memberships, special interest groups, languages spoken or relevant personal activities that might positively impact on a board appointment.

REFEREES

This section lists your referee's details as they can influence a board when making an appointment. Ideally your referees would be at board level. It is important not to include contact details for your referees.

9 YOUR 'BOARD-READY' COVERING LETTER

There is a temptation by some not to write cover letters. The reality is that cover letters are a valuable resource often carefully read by chairs and recruiters alike. A strong cover letter demonstrates that you have more to offer than just what is on your CV. However, for a cover letter to be of real value it needs to be both accessible and readable.

In the past, cover letters were often deemed to be 'good enough' if they simply introduced you and your interest in the role advertised and then referred to your attached CV. As a result, they were often too brief, functional at best and added no additional value. For this reason, they were rarely read. In a post GFC and competitive labor market, cover letters form a crucial part of your non-executive application process, regardless of whether you are responding to an advertisement, using a recruiter or approaching a company directly.

A GOOD COVER LETTER

Content aside, a good cover letter should be:

Accessible. Because your cover letter is important and you want it read, you should submit it in the body of your e-mail application or as part of your CV document - not as a separate attachment (if applicable). By doing so, it is much more likely to be read and, as such, distinguish you from other applicants.

Readable. It should never be more than a single page long. To keep it succinct, readable and relevant.

Key Ideas

You might like to consider including the following paragraphs in your cover letter:

Passion For the role. The first paragraph must grab the attention of the reader. Chair, recruiters and appointment/nomination committees look for applicants who are intelligent, qualified and passionate about what they do. So, this paragraph's not a statement about your understanding of the company, where you saw the job advertised or what the role is that you are applying for. Instead, it must demonstrate your passion for the role. It is where your earlier research begins to pay dividends (more on this topic later). This kind of opening can be incredibly powerful. Firstly, it immediately captures the reader's attention. It then demonstrates, from the outset, a number of positive qualities - your enthusiasm for the role, your ability to do it, your intelligence, connectedness and that you have done more research than most other applicants. All of which demonstrates you to be a proactive and motivated applicant. It is a strong start.

Your profile. The profile you should have already written as part of your CV. To recap, it summarizes your experience, your success, your networks, your achievements and your education and should be inserted as your second paragraph. It is OK to duplicate this information because you do not want this information overlooked. It is your answer to the question *'Why should the board appoint me?'*

Address gaps or concerns. It is not uncommon for boards to disregard an applicant because of a misinformed interpretation or assumption based on a poorly crafted CV. So, this paragraph should briefly allay any fears the Chair or Nominations Committee might have regarding your application so that they do not discount you. To head off any assumptions, you should try to ensure you are absolutely clear about any issues or gaps in your CV. For example, perhaps you are a contractor and change jobs frequently as part of your career plan. Unless told otherwise, the reader of your CV could interpret this as your inability to commit to an organisation. In this case, you should state clearly why you change roles so frequently. In a board context, you might be a CEO and part of the board. Unless you state this explicitly it will probably be assumed that you were not part of the board.

Ideally, this is a very short paragraph. It might address issues such as the belief that: you are too old, too young, over-experienced, under-experienced, it is your first board role, you have what some might consider too many board roles already or you have a perceived conflict of interests, etc. Equally, if there is something in your past that should be addressed, address it here and explain yourself rather than have others make assumptions perhaps not based on the full facts.

What is memorable about you? The reality is that boards want comfort and to be able to positively announce their new appointments. As such, you need to demonstrate that you will fit in, but also provide something for them to remember you by - it could make the difference between your appointment or not.

Begin by asking yourself the question *'Whom would you appoint to a board if you had to make a decision between two or more equally qualified candidates?'* The individual who seemed to have a personality, who would fit culturally into the board and had demonstrated their achievements outside of work (clubs, sporting achievements, languages etc.) or those who could not demonstrate any interests or success outside of a work setting and seemed the same as everyone else?

Passion for the company. This is one of the most important sections of your cover letter but different from your opening paragraph. It should be based on your previous research.

This summary paragraph demonstrates your understanding of what the company does, your connectedness, intelligence and strategic approach. Most importantly, it demonstrates your passion for the objectives or goals of the organisation. It is a strong way to finish any cover letter.

10 BOARD APPOINTMENTS

Like much in life, there is the theory on the one hand and, on the other hand, the actual practice.

Many senior executive appointment processes are tied to a rigid format. However, the board appointment process is often a more personal and flexible affair that is highly reliant upon personal connections. The recommendations and knowledge that stem from these relationships carry significant gravitas. This is important to understand and should shape the way you look at and apply for board positions.

I have seen perfectly good candidates be disregarded because of one negative comment made by a board member. For example, I have been in a board appointment meeting and listened to a board member state that he had heard that a particular candidate, while working with an ex colleague, almost 10 years ago, in a more junior position, was not a great leader. This is a tenuous critique when delivered by a board colleague meant that the candidate's application was for all intents and purposes disregarded.

Whilst many appointment processes are more flexible than their executive counterparts a relatively small, but growing, proportion of boards are also using executive search firms (headhunters) to find new board members. This process is generally more considered and thorough though are equally susceptible to closing early.

Additionally, a small proportion of Government boards or committees use search firms and/or advertise. These processes usually stick rigidly to application forms and timings. Though being a 'known candidate' still carries a great deal of weight.

While, you should not ignore the formal processes of advertising, director's registers (www.boarddirection.com.au) or executive search firms, remember that even within those more formal processes, personal networks will play a critical part. This makes broadening your own network and sending a message out through your personal connections, that you are looking for a board role, one of the most important steps in finding and securing a board position.

In summary, having worked in board recruitment and seeing the board appointment process in practice for almost 10 years, in my experience there are four ways individuals are appointed to a board. They are through:

- **Personal connections (networking)**
- **Advertisements**
- **Executive search firms (headhunters/recruiters)**
- **A direct approach**

The following chapters look at each of these four appointment processes in detail and provide practical advice in how to navigate each of them effectively.

11 DEVELOPING PERSONAL CONNECTIONS

A recent study I conducted found that almost 70% of all board appointments are made via personal connections - so this is where you should begin. This chapter considers this challenge as well as providing some practical advice on how to develop those personal connections.

If indeed people are being appointed to boards 70% of the time through connections, but you are spending 100% of your time responding to job adverts or using headhunters, then you need to reconsider your approach.

SERENDIPITY

People talk about chance meetings changing their lives. In fact, if you look back on the significant moments of your life, you can often see that 'chance' that got you where you are today. I am not much one for 'chance' but even I recognize that serendipity has played a significant role in the careers of many -not least of which mine.

The simple reality of developing personal connections is that the more you do it the more you increase the 'chance' of those chance meetings which might change your life -or get you on a board that you hadn't even considered.

For example, as a headhunter I know that despite my hard work and dedicated searches for the 'right' board candidate serendipity, played an enormous role in the board appointment process. I regularly found that having been given a new board role to fill it was often the candidate that I met recently by chance that would be appointed.

Don't get me wrong. I am not complaining. I would never have found them in my standard search. Instead, I learnt quickly of the value in meeting people, even people that I initially thought were not worth seeing, because I just never knew how valuable that meeting might be for the future.

By way of an example, I remember seeing one individual with a very specific set of skill that I had never had to recruit for. The next day a client asked me to find an individual with those exact skills. Because of my chance meeting, I could help immediately - good for me, good for the client and good for the candidate - serendipity!

THE REASON FOR DEVELOPING PERSONAL CONNECTIONS

For the reasons above, and many more, developing personal connections should be an essential part of your board search process. Here are just a few of the reasons I think doing so is key.

1. You get to meet people. These people, just as you are, are gateways to new relationships which you can benefit from in any number of social or financial ways.

2. You find out information. Information really is power - the more interlinked people you know and the information you know about the roles/organizations you are applying for the better chance you will have of being appointed. The opposite is true as well!

3. You can generate new spheres of knowledge. This broadens your influence and access to information that hadn't been presented to you by your current connections

4. You can contribute to others. Others need your knowledge, connections and relationships to prosper just as much as you need theirs.

5. It can get you appointed to a board. I think it has been mentioned already that I found that almost 70% of all board appointments are made via personal connections.

OLD SCHOOL NETWORKS

Let's tackle the elephant in the room: Many ask, *'Aren't most board appointments made via old school networks?'*

Yes and No. As discussed earlier, most boards appoint members partly based on the connections they bring to the organisation. These connections may be used to increase the knowledge of the board or bring new business opportunities, but can equally, and rightly, be used to strengthen the board's makeup.

While it is true that many boards leverage their existing networks to form shortlists to fill vacancies and this practice is facilitated by 'old boys club' relationships, this is not always a bad thing. A board's social fabric is often quite delicate and existing board members are very aware of this. They are also, arguably, in the best position to know what kind of candidate would be best suited to the board. For this reason, and in my experience, most boards when faced with a vacancy first ask board members if they know of anyone suitable to join the board. If someone is recommended, this can often be the end of the 'search'. Failing this approach, or to complement it, a formal process may also be undertaken with these personal recommendations thrown into the mix.

It is sometimes leveled at a board that they are using a formal process to rubber stamp an already chosen individual. I rarely find this to be the case. Most often I find that boards advertise a vacancy or use a search firm to genuinely test the market or compare a favored individual with other interested parties.

Looking at the board appointments process critically and in comparison to an executive appointment, many would see lots of similarities -even across sectors. Using personal connections to fill executive roles is just as commonly used by not for profit organizations, government bodies and private companies. In fact, if you were to be honest, you have probably been guilty of introducing people that you know for executive roles in the past too -and would do so again. I would.

So, do old boys networks count? Yes, absolutely, but no more than any other network. The trick is getting yourself part of them.

Who should you develop personal connections with?

The short answer is 'Everyone'.

There is a common phrase that says *'don't dress for your*

current role, dress for the role you aspire to'. A similar concept applies to developing personal connections you should build relationships with people that you admire and have the career that you aspire to. These people can often be found by researching the boards of organizations you are interested in.

However, whilst it is often tempting to only network with those you aspire to, you should not discount the value that the more mature or young have to offer. However, I have found that some of my most valuable connections have come via individuals who I never dreamt could help. Never judge an individual on first impressions and always be willing to give them your time.

WEAK TIES VERSUS STRONG TIES

Weak ties make you powerful. Malcolm Gladwell points to sociologist Mark Granovetter, whose classic study, *Getting a Job*, surveyed 282 Boston workers and found that 56% got jobs through a personal connection. Of those connections, most were weak ties. Only 16.7% saw the contact often, 55.6% saw them occasionally, and 28% saw them rarely. This means that people were nearly three times as likely to have found their job through a personal contact as through an advertisement, headhunter or other formal means. In other words, success is largely about who you know, not what you know.

This finding was magnified in my own study of board members, which found that almost 70% found their most recent board role via a personal connection. Whilst we did not survey whether these appointments were via strong or weak ties, extrapolating Granovetter's statistics might mean that up to 60% of all board appointments are made via personal connections that are seen 'occasionally' or 'rarely'.

If potentially 60% of people are finding board appointments

through their personal connections but you are spending 100% of your time responding to job adverts or working with headhunters, then you have to question whether this is the most effective use of your time.

The point here is, I hope, clear - personal connections work and when it comes to getting appointed to a board, weak ties are more important than strong ties.

Why are weak ties so effective?

A 'weak tie' is someone you see occasionally or rarely. 'Strong ties' on the other hand are people you see regularly and who occupy the same community that you do. The latter might work with you, live near you, go to the same churches or parties as you do. By association they are likely that they know of the same board opportunities that you do or assume that you know of these opportunities.

This situation is worsened when you take into consideration the Fundamental Attribution Error. If they do not know you are a board member, or interested in further opportunities, they may not bother telling you about the opportunities they know of or, if they do, you may already know about them.

The reason that 'weak ties' are so effective is because they are outside of your day-to-day activities. These people have, by definition, different connections to yours and are more willing to freshly evaluate what you do when you meet. This often results in new opportunities that you would not access through your 'strong ties'.

How do you develop 'weak ties'?

The trick here is to connect with as many 'weak ties' as possible, but start doing it via your strong ties. Here are some suggestions of ways to do this:

1. Begin with your close friends. Ask the question about whom they could introduce you to. Tell them you are looking for a board to sit on - be specific, be clear, be passionate. Get introductions - be bold.

2. Have a coffee with board directors that you know personally and let them know that you are looking for a non-executive role.

3. Get more involved in one or two community groups that offer networking opportunities.

4. Attend relevant conferences and seminars and make new contacts and revive old ones.

5. Do favors for others, make introductions, send articles, e-mail birthday wishes, make comments on blogs -be helpful. Get introductions -be bold.

6. Use LinkedIn. A great place to begin connecting with NEDs. From experience, most NEDs will give time to with anyone with a genuine passion or interest in serving on a board.

7. Find a Mentor/Connector or someone who knows people you want to know.

8. Start applying for roles. Board Direction (www.boarddirection.com.au) is a great place to start. Use it as a place to begin meeting other Board Directors looking to make appointments. Introduce yourself, introduce yourself to their competitors, introduce yourself to others on their boards or subcommittees, and speak with friends who may have/do work for them.

In summary 'weak ties' are more likely to know about board

roles you don't. They represent social power ó and the more you have, the more effective you will be in finding a board role. Developing your personal connections -strong and weak – is likely to be the most effective way to find a board position. Be aware though, that while taking the approach is more likely to land you a board role, it can be a slow journey. In fact, many experienced NEDs speak of this being a 12 month - 3-year exercise. You need to start now.

Consider the following when trying to develop personal connections:

1. Be clear. The 'Fundamental Attribution Error' (FAE) is linked closely with having a clear board message. Malcolm Gladwell writes about this in his best-selling book *'Tipping Point'*. He writes that *the* Fundamental Attribution Error stems from the fact that people *"instinctively want to explain the world around them in terms of people's essential attributes."* In other words, they do not consider the setting, culture or external influences, rather they focus on immediately graspable facts first.

For this reason, having a message that is too broad or encompasses a number of aspirations will negatively impact on how people view your board aspiration. This will in turn affect your ability to effectively leverage your personal connections into a board position.

In short, people have a difficulty in pegging people to more than one thing, so unless you are clear about what you want them to peg you against (i.e. you as a potential board member), they may not remember you at all or forget what you were trying to position yourself as. Therefore, having a clear message/board profile about your board aspirations is key.

2. Be persistent. Individuals who develop effective personal connections are persistent. Persistence comes through having a strong motivation. Motivated people see opportunities to network everywhere: at dinner parties, on planes, in the office, at your children's sporting events etc.

Motivation can be broken down in two ways: towards motivation & away from motivation.

Towards motivation suggests heading towards a particular goal. In a networking context, it could be that you want to meet other board members in order to become a board member yourself.

Away from motivation is different in that your motivation in doing something is in order not to feel a negative consequence. For example, you don't speed because you don't want to be caught speeding or you might be motivated to meet new people because you don't want to be stuck in the rut of your current role.

The seemingly small difference in motivation here is important because it plays out in how you interact with those you meet. Away from motivation does not lend itself to the passion that others find so attractive and I wrote about earlier. Instead, it is often embodied in 'needy' language '. I really want a board position' or 'no one will give me an opportunity'. This sort of language is debilitating for both the user and listener and will negatively impact on your effectiveness as a developer of personal connections.

3. Take the initiative. NEDs are often incredibly passionate about the work of the organizations on whose board they sit. This makes developing personal connections with NEDs a terrific experience and not nearly as intimidating as other forms of networking.

In my experience, experienced NEDs are up for a conversation about most things more often than anyone else and enjoy being introduced to new people. Furthermore, I have found that they are particularly willing to engage with relative strangers about what they do, how they do it, what their organisation does and about what the market for NEDs looks like.

Beyond their accessibility, another of the reasons that networking with NEDS is not as challenging as in an executive context is that the conversations you have with them are unlikely to end with a 'hard sell' -unlike when people are looking for full-time work or are trying to sell a product.

Furthermore, there is a common belief that serving on a board is about 'giving something back'. For this reason, board directors enjoy helping others to contribute in a similar fashion to the way they do.

Finally, most NEDs recognize that the foundation for their past and future board career is based on who they know -as much as what they know. They see value in having diverse relationships because through them new opportunities present themselves.

In the end, you get out what you put in. So take the initiative, introduce yourself to someone new and enjoy yourself - what is the worst that could happen?

4. Be genuine. In addition to being clear, being authentic is essential to any successful networking process and will help you enjoy the process of meeting people more. For example, if you are an inexperienced or aspirational board member, then genuinely asking others with more board experience for their advice is an easy 'in'. Don't pretend to be someone you are not - you don't need to be the most experienced person in the room all the time. Conversely, if you have board experience already, then you can trade on this experience to develop new relationships with other NEDs. Sharing war stories or common challenges for boards is a great way to get a conversation started. Furthermore, having something in common is a great way to bond with a new connection.

5. Be passionate. I have mentioned 'passion' in this book almost as much as I have mentioned the value of developing personal connections. But, what should you be passionate about? In truth, it does not really matter. Whether it is the passion you have for board work, the industry you are in, what you do outside of work or what you can contribute. All are equally appealing to a listener. Knowing what it is you love doing and how to explain it is the key.

6. How can you help? 'How can I help?' is almost a mantra that I have in my head whenever I am in the room with people I don't know.

Showing a genuine interest in what others do and how they got to do it is a powerful approach to developing meaningful connections. I like to ask questions of others, listen to what they say and see if I can help as a result.

Often the best way to help is by introducing them to others who know more about an issue than maybe you do, or someone who works in their industry but they don't know. Equally, freely sharing what and whom you know and giving (quality) advice is a useful approach. Taking this approach, I believe, is the right thing to do, but also presents a great excuse to keep in touch and to endear yourself.

7. Be curious. You don't always have to be the smartest person in the conversation. Believing this can open the opportunity for you to be genuinely curious about others. I am always interested to know what people know that I don't. I am just as interested to find out why they know it and I don't. This doesn't make you vulnerable, rather it empowers the conversation and this new knowledge can invariably be leveraged in future conversations.

8. Be prepared. It should now be apparent that the opportunity to develop new personal contacts can happen at any time. For this reason, you need to be prepared to take advantage of the opportunity when it strikes.

Ensure that you have business cards and a pen on you at all times. The reason for the first is obvious, i.e. should you have the opportunity to exchange cards you are able to do so. Having a pen on hand is valuable because you can write on the card to remind you of the context in which it was received and any useful facts that came about through the conversation -like any introductions you promised to make or personal attributes.

While many might perceive that business cards are dated, the majority of NEDs still carry them and expect others to do the same. Beyond this I find most people enjoy the formality of exchanging contact information in this fashion and feel it appropriately formal to mean something more than a handshake.

9. Follow through and follow up. Do what you said you would.

Surprisingly, studies have shown 'successful' leaders - leaders who get things done - are not necessarily the most outgoing, gregarious, smartest or have the strongest interpersonal skills. Instead, most successful leaders do one thing. They follow through. If they say they will do something, they do it.

Putting yourself in the category of strong leaders means that you need to follow through on the promises you make while networking. For example, if you promised an introduction or to e-mail through an article, make sure you do so.

Equally, the follow up is as important as the follow through. If you have made an introduction, then wait a week or two and follow it up. Ask both parties how they found the meeting you set up and whether you can help any further. If it was an article you sent through, find out how it was received.

Successful leaders know that this approach works - now you do!

10. Start a habit. Developing personal connections is not something everyone enjoys doing. Hopefully, the points above will increase your motivation to do this and have provided some practical suggestions for making it easier.

In the end, just getting out there and meeting people will feel more comfortable if you do it regularly. So, get in the habit of introducing yourself to others and offering to help in the knowledge that it can only get easier.

11. Ask for what you want. Finally, just meeting with people won't help you with your board aspirations unless you have a clear goal in mind.

To help you capitalize on the opportunities you have, it is useful to have a couple of questions that stem from your ultimate goal of finding board opportunities. Perhaps ask *'who do you know who I should know given (your circumstance)'*, or *'who do you know who might know'*.

I find this sort of questioning encompasses many outcomes you are hoping for when developing personal connections, i.e. it gives the conversation a purpose; it provides something to speak about; it provides an appropriate platform to address your curiosity and shows that you are genuinely interested in what they do.

12 THE VALUE OF (GOOD) RESEARCH

Research is by far the most important element of any application or job-hunting process. Though, conversely, it is probably the most under-utilized, and the most difficult, element to motivate yourself to undertake - it is even harder to do well. However, doing so will assist you in submitting a stronger and more informed application than your competitors and this will increase your chances of being appointed.

Thorough research should take the shape of four separate activities. They are:

1. Desk research. Most people consider research something desk-based and primarily done online. If at all, it is rarely done more than twice by most applicants. In a typical application or job-hunting process this research is initially done when a job/board opportunity is first noticed, and then secondly, immediately before an interview.

Whilst Internet research is not useless (far from it), taking this approach will not differentiate you from any other applicant, which is the whole point of your application process -to separate you from other applicants and therefore be appointed. Instead, the principle of online or desk-based research is that it should only be undertaken as a starting point for more in-depth research.

2. Personal research. Often the research that is most effective can only be gained by leaving your computer and experiencing what the organisation does directly. Where possible, try to visit the organisation in person to get a feel for the culture, setup and size. Failing this, do some mystery shopping, use their website, call the administration or HR team, buy a product or use their service.

Some of my most impressive candidates have done all these things and referenced them in interviews and applications to great effect. The reason it is so effective is because no-one else does it. It shows a proactive approach to understanding the organisation -something most boards want in board members.

3. Speak to people. Try and speak to someone you know who may have worked at the organisation or who may be able to introduce you to a person who does. If this doesn't work and you cannot find anybody on the 'inside' to speak with, speak to the organization's competitors or their stakeholders and ask them what they think of the organization's services/products, or their perceived strengths and weaknesses. Alternatively, just introduce yourself to someone you don't know that works there.

Researching applications are a great excuse to speak with your peers or, better still, to the peers of the organisation who might appoint you. A particularly effective approach can be to phone them (your peers), and tell them that you are thinking of applying to sit on the board of a particular organisation and you were hoping that they might be able to provide a perspective on whether they think it is a good role for you.

This can be a daunting approach for many, but by taking it you will have proven a couple of things: you will have generated a new connection or renewed an old one and you will have gained invaluable insight into the workings of the organisation and on the boar of the organisation you wish to serve and finally, you will have equipped yourself to put in a stronger application. I can almost guarantee, that this personal research is something that will continue to separate you from other applicants throughout the process.

4. Contact about the opportunity. The final element of your research culminates in the phone call to the search firm or advertiser of the role. Only after completing your desk-based and personal research should this occur. By doing your research first you can now begin to differentiate yourself from other applicants - here you are beginning the process of 'daring them not to interview you' (more later).

Referencing your research and actions in this phone call is a powerful approach and can ensure that you stand out from the other applicants who might just call and ask generically about the role.

This approach is particularly effective when dealing with recruiters and even more so when you are dealing directly with the company or its chair because it makes you memorable.

Isn't this too much?
Many people worry about doing this level of research. Either they feel they are abusing the application process or are worried about making themselves known for fear of what might be said about them without their permission.

The first point is a valid one. You certainly do not want to be seen to be unfairly influencing the appointment decision, but this can be overcome if you approach those you speak with, with a clear desire to inform yourself about the role/organisation rather than seeking to influence the decision-making process.

The second point should not concern you. If you do your research properly, and represent yourself well, then you will be represented well. In fact, getting people to speak warmly about you is exactly what you want to happen in an application process. It gives you an advantage at the short-listing stage and in interviews, because you become a 'known product' and, as such, potentially also a much more attractive candidate.

Know what you know

Having finished your research (which should take a couple of days,) you should have all the information you need to complete an application that stands out. By undertaking research beyond that which you get from in front of a computer, you will have likely found out:

- What is important to the company?
- Who the decision-makers are?
- What the role demands?
- What it is like working there?
- How the company functions?
- About their products and services?
- Who their clients are?
- Who their competitors are?

Again, by doing this level of research you will be *'daring them not to interview you'* and demonstrating yourself to be proactive and intelligent and thereby presenting better than other applicants.

13 BOARD ADVERTISEMENTS

COMPETITION

Finding a board position is a highly competitive exercise -you need to dare them not to appoint you.

When looking for board positions most people treat advertised vacancies as the holy grail of job hunting, often dedicating all their time looking for and responding to them. Bearing in mind that relatively few board seekers find positions this way, it is arguably a most depressing and unproductive use of your time. Having mentored many people through the board search process I know how frustrating it can be receiving 'thanks but no thanks' letters or no letter at all in response to your applications. However, despite the low success rates, this is still an important element for any board hunter to get right.

What should you do?

Firstly, you should know that existing relationships and informal networks often count more than the stated application process itself. With this in mind, it is important to know what to expect when responding to a board vacancy - even one that is advertised.

Organizations always want the best people to sit on their

board but the process for finding them can be daunting for them and the resources required often under-estimated. Because of this, the process can often be abruptly altered, as stated application date closed early or the appointment instead made via a personal connection at the expense of the stated process.

Whilst I believe holding out for a stated closing date to finish is good PR for an organisation and valuable (as often the last few applications received are the best ones), an organisation managing their own appointment process may view things differently. You can imagine a formal, long and resource sapping process stopping early occurring if, for example, one hundred applications had been received and there were still two more weeks until applications formally closed. It would equally be likely to happen if some of the applications that were already received were deemed 'good enough'. And, more likely still if someone connected to the board recommended a candidate that they thought was appropriate.

The situation described above occurs more often than you might think and has left many a disappointed potential applicant. This flexibility can happen for very good reasons and should not be used as an indication of the quality of the board or organization. Instead, it should guide the way you approach application processes. So, what is the take away here?

Don't wait too long to apply

Get your application in early, clarify the process and register an interest (immediately after doing your research) when you find an opportunity. In short, you want to be the first applicant they receive an application from that is 'good enough'.

14 THE APPLICATION ITSELF

Having done your research and deciding to apply for a position in response to an advert, it is important to know that many board applications often have guidelines. This may seem obvious but many people do not know that applications have rules, and even fewer take the time to understand or adhere to them.

Ignoring these guidelines can negatively impact how your application is received and your chances of successfully being appointed. In some cases, it can lead to your application not even being considered!

RULES FOR APPLYING TO BOARDS

Structuring your application for a board role by adhering to the instructions is therefore essential. By doing so, your application will more likely be in a style that the organisation is familiar with and as such will be more readable and more often read.

How do you find these rules and what are they?

Regardless of what kind of director role you are applying for, it is good practice to contact the organisation or individual receiving the application before applying. When applying for a position the organisation itself, or the recruitment firm, are often the keepers of these guidelines as they pertain to their client's/the organization's application requirements. They will know in what style they like their applications to be received and what content should be contained within.

Ask questions

The purpose of your call is to understand what your application should contain and what the key areas are that you should address. You might want to ask: *'How should I apply?'* or *'What would you like from me by way of an application?'* or, alternatively, *'What are the key areas you would like me to address in my application?'*

Asking questions like the ones above ensure that you understand what is required in a written application. This is important because, particularly in more formal application processes, those who do not submit their applications per the guidelines risk having their applications disregarded. While this may seem petty, I cannot tell you how often a seemingly qualified applicant has applied for a role but has not been shortlisted because they did not follow carefully specified application processes. So regardless of your seniority you need to 'join the circus' and jump through the hoops set out before you.

Know what they don't want

You should also be able to find out what they don't want. This is equally important, because if a comprehensive application is not warranted and a brief CV is all that is required, then it is useful to know that before you submit a lengthy application that may be only skimmed through.

Address the essential criteria

If there is a list of essential criteria -unless directed otherwise you should address them all. Even if you feel as if you are duplicating your responses, you need to continue to address them each specifically.

These do not need to be lengthy responses -remember it needs to be readable. First and foremost, you need to demonstrate, not that you have done what they are asking, but that you have done it successfully. So, you need to include both what you have done and evidence of success (or at the very least the board's evidence of success).

In fact, some of the most powerful responses I have seen here have simply been a list of 'evidence of success' - don't be afraid of being brief. Your cover letter should make up for this.

If all else fails

As a rule, if no specific information is requested by way of an application you should submit your tailored board CV and a cover letter addressed to the chair.

15 EXECUTIVE SEARCH FIRMS

Having worked in this realm for almost 10 years, my advice is that, wherever possible you should not rely on search firms to find yourself a board position. I say this <u>only</u> because if they are speaking to you, then they are speaking to hundreds of people just like you -that is of course their job! In doing so, they are placing you in direct competition with other candidates, reducing your chances of getting the role you want.

Meeting with an executive search firm to express interest in getting a board appointment can be a useful intelligence-gathering exercise though it seldom yields direct results. That said, serendipity does come into play more often than you might think and you might get your timing right. But many who rely on this approach to find a board position wait by the phone in vain.

Perhaps too far at the end of the spectrum was an experienced ASX 200 Board Member whom I met recently who stated that *'headhunters are not your friends'*. Whilst this may sometimes be true, the reality is that they are far more powerful than many give them credit for and should be treated as friends regardless of your feelings. Furthermore, even 'bad' headhunters are gatekeepers to the board positions that you want.

HOW TO WORK WITH RECRUITERS

No matter how you feel about working with recruiters you need to know how to do so effectively.

Power

Recruiters are powerful because they are listened to by the decision-makers on the board that you want to be appointed to.

A common misconception is that the role of a headhunter is just to pass CVs to the board. In reality, most headhunters are hand-picked by the board because they have developed, often over a long period of time, a close relationship with a board member(s) - your potential colleagues. For this reason, they are often seen as 'trusted advisors' and they are asked their opinion on the candidates they put forward - their opinions therefore count.

I have been in many boardrooms where I have been asked my opinion on board candidates because I am trusted by individuals on the board and, by association, the board as a whole. Whether you like it or not, my opinion, as a headhunter, counts!

Some of the questions I am often asked include:
1. Have I met or spoken to the candidate (and what I think)?
2. Do I know of anyone who knows them?
3. What their reputation is like?
4. How they performed in their previous roles?
5. What I really think (off the record)?
6. Who I would appoint?

In the case that I know or have spoken with the candidate, I can answer these questions and my answers are powerful 'nudges' towards or away from an appointment.

Motivation

Executive search firms are retained by their clients to find candidates to serve as directors on boards, not to find board positions for candidates. This is an important motivation to recognize and should influence the way you interact with search consultants (headhunters).

Search firms work in a number of different ways, but essentially they are advertisers for vacancies, in that they are paid to attract candidates. Their success and reputation is built on providing as many qualified candidates for the role as they can.

There are always exceptions, but most firms are interested in making as many placements as they can, which means submitting as many quality candidates as they can for as many roles as possible. For this reason, their focus is not always about finding the best person for the job, instead it is primarily about making a placement.

Reputation

In many ways, recruiters do not differ much from an employer or an HR team - they are motivated to succeed because their reputation depends on it. If you want to use recruiters effectively, then, perversely perhaps, it is in your best interest to try to improve their reputation.

Think of it this way. Would you recommend a friend for a job in a company you worked for if you knew that your reputation would be likely to suffer because of it? Probably not. Likewise, a recruiter who does not know you won't recommend or stick their neck out for you unless they are fully convinced you are going to make them look good. Therefore, if you can impress them, they will be more willing and able to impress their client on your behalf. Conversely, if they are not impressed by you and feel that their reputation might be harmed, they will be less likely to recommend you.

This means that you need to assure them that you are the most highly qualified, most knowledgeable, most presentable and most affable candidate. If you can do this, then they are likely to personally support your application - a powerful thing.

In summary, using an executive search firm is an important element of a comprehensive board search process and can lead to results -especially for the most senior of board opportunities. Be sure you understand how to work with headhunters, what their motivations are and

HOW TO USE EXECUTIVE SEARCH FIRMS EFFECTIVELY

Search firms typically manage only a small proportion of board vacancies and there is not one firm who manage the majority of these. Often, these firms complement their search processes with an advertisement. When this occurs, it is not uncommon for these advertisements and the search to generate hundreds of applications. It is not surprising to find then that relatively few individuals find roles by responding to by working through these firms. However, there are many individuals out there -not just the 'great and the good' - who do find working with search firms to get a board position.

Still, with a relatively low placement rate to the applications received it is worth spending time considering how to work with search firms effectively.

To recap, search firms are, amongst other things, 'gatekeepers' that need to be navigated past to get to decision-makers. This usually requires an application process of some description. The following sets out how to use search firms effectively when applying for a board position.

Research, Research & Research

Here it is again in case you missed it earlier: The research process is about gathering enough information to impress the search consultant so that they feel comfortable impressing the client on your behalf. You need to do a number of things like:

1. **Desk-based research** -Google, website analysis, etc.

2. **Speak with people** you know who know the organisation.

3. **Call the client's organisation** or do some 'mystery shopping'.

4. **Visit the organisation** or use the facilities/services offered by them.

Impress them

If you do your research and you get this right, then you cannot help but impress. It will clearly separate you from your competitors and in turn give the recruiter the incentive to impress their client on your behalf.

But remember, if you fail to impress or are not ready for the meetings or phone calls ahead, then your lack of preparedness may generate a negative referral. This can all but ruin your chance of a successful placement. Perversely, I think that the fear of this happening is, I suspect, one of the reasons many poor candidates do not do this level of research.

Call to gain information

The key to any successful assignment is a search firm first taking a full brief from their client. This is information that you as an applicant do not always have access to but you need to know. It is possible to get it from other sources, but having this information straight from those who are making the recruitment decisions is invaluable.

You should treat the call to a recruiter as the first, and arguably most powerful, step in your application process. Again, if you can impress them, then they are likely to impress the client on your behalf. But do it right!

On countless occasions a potential applicant has called me and said *'I saw the advert for X. Can you tell me about the role?'* without having done any research or giving any thought to their suitability. My initial response used always to be *'Have you read the job description yet?'* or *'Have you looked at their website?'* Most hadn't, and not having done so was embarrassing for them, because they knew they should have before calling. Those who were not embarrassed, based on that poor conversation, put themselves behind those who, instead of ringing me immediately, did some research first.

Some of the most impressive calls have begun with something like this:

'Hello. My name is (insert name here). I saw the advert for the board position at BCD. I have had a look at their website and have spoken to some of their stakeholders including Mr. X, Mrs. Y & Organisation Z. I even managed to get an introduction to their Chief Executive from a mutual friend. I understand that one of the issues BCD might be facing at board level is about the impact that the strong dollar has on their overseas businesses. Is that right? Also, if I tell you a little about myself could you tell me a little more about the role and whether you think my skill set matches what you are looking for?'

This is an impressive start to any conversation. Sure, it requires some research but it will be worth it for all the reasons I have mentioned before. Even if you only do half the research required to have this conversation, it will still put you above all the other candidates who haven't done this.

Ask good question

Some of the better questions I have received include:

1. Why is the organisation looking for a new board member?
2. Why did the previous incumbent leave?
3. What is the culture of the board like?
4. What are the aspirations of the board?
5. Is there an internal /preferred candidate?
6. How should I apply and what would you like from me by way of an application?

Questions like those above separate you from the mundane applicant who asks about money or the same questions as everyone else. They demonstrate you to be intelligent, informed and in tune with what an organisation might want.

They are not presumptuous nor are they arrogant. Instead they are sensible and, importantly, they suggest that you know your value and do not want to have your time wasted - they speak of your 'gravitas'.

Stay close

From experience, those who know and have a strong affinity with a search firm are more likely to be recommended for roles by that firm. Conversely where the firm or the board do not personally know the candidate, these applicants quickly slip down the 'must see' list.

Headhunters are human - it may not always seem that way, but they are - and because they see and speak to so many people, it is quite possible that they might forget you or that your application is 'lost' during a busy period or hectic schedule. You cannot afford for this to happen. So, for the reasons above, you need to ensure that you stay at the forefront of the mind of the recruiter who is managing your application. How do you do this? As a candidate, you should always look to add value to your application by helping the search consultant. You can do this in a number of ways including:

1. **Trying to find leads** that you can pass on to the consultant - this gives you an excuse to call them again and you will be seen favorably by them.
2. **Continuing your research** - this gives you more excuses to call when you find out new pieces of information that need clarity or the consultant might be interested in.
3. **Introducing friends** who are looking for new board work - introducing them to the consultant works because it is an opportunity for them to find new clients or candidates. Alternatively, providing business development leads is a great way to develop rapport.
4. **Finally, try to meet the recruiter personally** - this can be tricky and in some cases be seen as 'too much' from the consultant's perspective but, if possible and appropriate, it is worth meeting them - offering to buy them a coffee or lunch helps.

Search firms trade on reputation and contacts. If you can help them with both, they will appreciate it and you will build a bond with them whilst simultaneously demonstrating you are well connected and intelligent. This can only be a good thing when you are in a competitive application process.

16 APPROACHING BOARDS DIRECTLY

A recent study I conducted showed that, of the board members surveyed (over 1000) that between 10% - 20% of people were appointed to their current board after approaching that company directly with the explicit intention of gaining a position on the board. The statistics are a little hazy only because I believe that there is some overlap with personal connections here (also an area I surveyed). That said, this approach to finding a role is, I believe, on a par with the combined success that you will have in working with search firms & responding to advertisements.

The underlying principle and strength of approaching an organisation directly is the same as that of networking yourself into a board position. It will separate you from other potential candidates and therefore you can avoid being one of hundreds applying for a role.

For this reason, you should treat approaching an organisation directly in a similar fashion to that of both networking and working with search firms. This chapter will, as a result, naturally blend some of the processes that the networking and search firm chapters covered - with a few key differences.

Specifically, the key difference in approaching organizations directly, compared to working with search firms or your networks, is that you are likely to have only 'one bite at the cherry'. By this I mean that you are likely to be dealing directly with the decision-makers and almost immediately!

HOW TO APPROACH DIRECTLY

Who should you speak to?

Unlike working with a search firm or responding to an advert, this approach requires you to speak directly to board members or the chair. It is unlikely that you would approach a board via a generic contact number for the organisation. Instead, you should be reaching out directly to a board member or, ideally, the Chair. Speaking to anyone other than a board member is likely to reflect badly on your ability to serve on the board because it suggests that you do not have the contacts or perhaps confidence or gravitas to work at board level.

Research

Like much of the prior advice, successful appointments often begin with strong research. Here, more than in any of your prior approaches, you are trying to dare the board not to see you directly. So, it is of utmost importance that you are prepared to do so from your first conversation. Before you begin to approach the company and in preparation for the first conversation, you should find out:

Who is on the board?
Ask yourself if you have any mutual contacts that might be able

to introduce you? Have you worked in similar fields to any of the board members? How would you fit on the board?

Who should you approach?
Ideally it would be the Chair. If not, then another board member might be appropriate, particularly if you know one member and can get a warm introduction and recommendation.

Research the individual that you will be speaking to
It is likely that you won't know or be connected to board members directly. If you do, that is good. You will have an easier conversation. If not, then you should research the background of that individual thoroughly. This can assist you in being considered a 'warm candidate' and forming a closer relationship with them - and as such having a greater chance of being appointed.

Research the board itself
Like researching the individual you will be approaching, you should also understand the skills matrix of the board. Try to ascertain what, if any, skill gaps the board might have or what skills they have too many of. Also, understand the tenure of board members -which members are due to retire first and what are the skills they bring to the board that you might be able to replace.

Research the organisation
You will likely be approaching an organisation specifically because you know what they do and think you can contribute. So, in one sense, your research here should be fairly straight forward and will not involve lengthy research.

However, it can still take some time and you should not short suit yourself by not knowing for example:

- Who the major stakeholders and competitors are
- What media activity is circulating about the organisation
- Their major economic challenges
- What the board is likely to be dealing with on a monthly basis.

This sort of research is likely to mean more research than you might be used to, but having this knowledge when it comes to approaching the board, can be invaluable. Again, speak with competitors, stakeholders, do some mystery shopping or speak to people that may have worked there in the past to get this information.

Use your networks - strong and weak

Speak to people in and around the board. Get a sense of what they do, what others think of them and work out if you have any mutual connections.

Mutual connections are powerful - they transform you from a 'cold applicant' to a 'warm applicant' so you need to work hard to become one, as they are more likely to be appointed.

If you don't know anyone, then you should consider introducing yourself to strangers (think 'Weak Ties'). The purpose here is not blatantly to get the role but instead to make yourself known and liked by them and their contacts. Again, LinkedIn is a powerful and convenient way to do this.

The Approach

Once you have completed your research, you should then have the confidence to introduce yourself. You can do this initially via e-mail, phone or social media (LinkedIn). Use the techniques outlined in the personal connections (networking) section of this book to find some language to use to introduce yourself and what you are proposing.

In an initial phone conversation/e-mail, it is often too confronting to get into the detail of what you are proposing. Instead, when you introduce yourself, ask if you could sit down over a coffee to discuss how you might be able to contribute to the organisation. Alternatively, arrange another time to have a discussion. Keep that initial call/e-mail brief and perhaps end your intro with something like *'Is that a conversation that would be worth having?'*

You only have one shot at impressing by taking this approach, so make sure you are prepared to do so. Should you be able to secure a meeting, you of course, need to be clear about what it is you have to offer to the board and organization's future.

You will need to be clear of your USP and why you have approached this particular individual in the first place.

The sort of responses to these questions will be determined a great deal by the findings of your research. For example, it could be that you have noticed a potential vacancy on the board or a gap in the skills matrix that you could fill.

If the conversation goes well, then, congratulations. All your hard work should have paid off. However, it is perfectly possible that they may not have an opportunity or the opportunity is 'not you, yet'. In any case say thank you, make an introduction to someone else that might be able to help or would be better on the board than even you.

The important thing here is to ensure that following any meeting/phone call, the board member is left with a positive view of what you can do and your ability to help.

This is likely to pay off in the future -whether it be this board or one just like it that, comes from a referral. Again, in any case you have made a new connection and one that if you maintain, can be a strong ally for what you do.

17 THE BOARD INTERVIEW

The secret to having a successful board interview is, again, preparation. Truth be told, if you have followed all the steps outlined in previous chapters: researching more than just the website, writing a board resume that demonstrates your successes, writing a cover letter using the 5 paragraphs outlined and really leveraging your strong and weak ties, then the interview should be a fairly straightforward affair.

APPROACHES USED TO IMPRESS

There a couple of approaches that I have found that successful candidates use to really impress. They are:

They present positively. Many studies of the recruitment industry suggest that interviewers make decisions about who to appoint within the first 5 minutes of an interview -some even say that it happens within 60 seconds. In any case, making a good first impression and having positive body language is important. With this in mind, you should:

They turn up early. Arriving late or immediately before an interview can mean that you feel rushed or on edge. This can impact on your body language, your conversations and on the way you are perceived by the interviewer. By arriving early, you are in the best position to put yourself in the right frame of mind for the forthcoming interview.

They are polite. I spoke to a colleague who was interviewing for a senior management role. On arrival, the candidate was rude to one of the security guards. Unbeknownst to them the security guard was good friends with my colleague and told her about this candidate's rudeness prior to the interview. My colleague proceeded to cancel the interview on the basis that if the candidate could not be polite to one of her staff they could not be trusted to represent the organisation appropriately. The lesson here? Be polite to everyone.

They dress appropriately. Ideally, dress a little above everyone's expectations. The dress culture of organizations differs dramatically, but I find that it is better to be overdressed than under -particularly for senior executive or NED roles.

Beyond 'looking good', you should also consider what is appropriate for an interview. I have had female interviewers comment on the 'inappropriate' amount of cleavage of some candidates. Likewise, I have had some candidates wear blue shirts and then proceed to sweat considerably -the outcome being big black splotches all over their shirt. Other candidates have worn excessive amounts of jewelry which makes a lot of noise during the interview. Here the issue is ensuring that the interviewer is concentrating on what you are saying rather than the color of your shirt, your cleavage or jewelry.

They consider their body language. A firm handshake is essential. Receiving a loose one is off-putting for interviewers. Likewise, an overly firm handshake can be intimidating.

Interviewers often imitate or respond to candidates based on what the candidates themselves are doing. A smiling candidate has a positive effect on the way that interviewers view candidates.

Show interest in the role by leaning forward a little with your hands in front of you. Leaning backwards or crossing your arms can appear defensive or signal a lack of interest.

They have researched the interviewer.
Really good candidates know that the recruitment process is a personal affair. They know that just demonstrating that they can do the role, have done the role in the past and can succeed in the role in the future is only part of what they need to do to be appointed.

For this reason, more and more candidates are beginning to research the people that are interviewing them -be that the Chair, the HR manager or the recruiter. Finding out as much as you can about these people's background and motivations can mean that it is easier to form a bond with them.

Achieving this bond means that it is more likely to get a positive review/recommendation of their performance because they are liked. Think of it this way. You are more likely to recommend someone for a role, and overlook any minor faults (which could ordinarily mean the difference between being appointed or not), if they are your friend or you like them.

I recommend at the very least Googling and searching the people interviewing you on LinkedIn to see where they have worked and what they are interested in. You can also find out easily (via LinkedIn) who in common you know and can then make mention of this in an interview. This approach potentially takes you from a 'cold' candidate to a 'warm' one and further improves your chances of being appointed.

They have researched the board & organisation.
This is obvious I hope. You should follow the earlier recommendations to ensure that you know what the motivations of the organisation and board are for finding a new NEDs.

The interview itself

Before entering any interview, you must know why you should be appointed. The first question you are likely to be asked in any interview (inferred or directly) is *'Why should you be appointed to the board?'* Having a clear answer to this in your mind is absolutely key.

Ideally, your response would replicate your board profile and should emphasize:
1. Your governance experience,
2. Your networks
3. Your passion for governance
4. What the organisation does and what executive skills you bring to the board.

T.E.A.

I recommend taking the TEA - T(echnical) E(xample) A(chievement) - approach to answering each interview question.

Technical
What is the technical or academic response to the question? For example, if asked about your understanding of governance you might say *'Governance is primarily based upon the fiduciary responsibility that a board of trustees has with respect to the exercise of authority over an organisation whilst serving the mission of the organization and those whom the organization serves.'*

Examples

Have examples to support your statements. Knowing why you should be appointed is the first step. To support your answers, you should also have a practical example of each of the four elements outlined in your profile. These examples would ideally be at board level, but could perhaps be in an executive context or gained by working with (not on) a board.

Achievements

Have evidence of your achievements at board level. The board appointment process is a competitive situation. To really stand out and to increase your chance of being appointed, you should have examples of achievements/success to support each of your board profile statements. Just responding with what you have done, makes you a 'B' candidate and, in a competitive environment, this is not good enough.

By definition, your successes as a NED are also those of the board. So, this is probably the most difficult part of any response, as often your board successes are not solely yours.

In this situation, I believe it is therefore ok to use the successes of the board as your own -whilst couching them as also being the board's successes. This means using as many details as possible. Ideally, you would have statistics or figures to demonstrate what you have done on the board or at least can demonstrate your involvement in key decisions and outcomes of the board. Think about the kind of issues you were involved in and what resolution was made. Also, think about your role on any subcommittees or other board services you provided beyond the role of governance.

This is the most challenging part of any interview. If you cannot evidence success at board level, then you need to ask yourself why you should be appointed to a board over others. It is clearly a critical part of the interview!

PITFALLS

In addition to the positive elements above, you should also be aware of some of the pitfalls that many, even good, candidates fall into. They include:

Over-answering. Whilst I have conducted formal interviews for as long as 2 hours, a typical interview ranges from 30 -60 minutes and contains approximately 10 questions. That means that after the initial meet and greet and some summary statements, you may have less than 5 minutes to answer each question and perhaps as little as 2 minutes.

Speaking too much and taking too long in an interview can reduce your impact dramatically for a number of reasons including:

1. Your point can get lost easily
2. You will likely be mixing your message
3. You will likely be answering future questions (and thus not the one you are asked
4. You bring into question your time management ability
5. You begin to bore the interviewer!

Being clear on why you should be appointed and taking the T.E.A approach to your responses, will mean that it is unlikely that you will speak too much and still answer the questions effectively.

If you feel like you are beginning to over-answer, look for clues. The biggest one to watch out for is if the interviewer has stopped writing. If this is the case, finish promptly and perhaps ask if there was more you could offer?

Asking too many questions. The reality is that by the end of the interview most interviewers will have made their mind up as to the appropriateness of the candidate. In this case, asking long or complex questions is likely only to negatively impact on their perception of you. Good candidates have most of the answers they need prior to attending an interview. Likewise, a good interview should provide answers to most of the questions that might usually be asked during the interview.

Keep in mind that interviewing can be exhausting and after conducting a number the interviewer will likely be getting tired. So, try to keep your questions brief or, better still, follow up the interview with an e-mail. Still, should all your essential questions not have been covered during the interview, you should ask them.

18 NON-EXECUTIVE INTERVIEW QUESTIONS

Every board interview is different. Some are formal (with the whole board) and some are done in a coffee shop (with just the Chair or consultant). However, in preparation for any interview you should consider what your response would be to the following questions that may be asked of you.

General Opening Questions
1. Can you briefly tell us a little about yourself and what synergies exist between your experience and that which is required by this board?
2. Why does this role appeal to you? Why are you considering it now?
3. What is your honest opinion of our organisation? What should we be doing differently?
4. Why should we appoint you to this board?

Governance Style
5. How hands on are you as a non-executive? To what extent are you interested in operational detail?
6. In your opinion, what conditions are absolutely necessary to ensure good governance?
7. What are the warning signs that usually precede a

breakdown in good governance?
8. What do you think the board's role is in relation to development of strategy?
9. How do you think the board should engage with executive management in this process?
10. Some directors thrive on working through challenging circumstances, but there is a point at which challenge can go too far. What are your thoughts on this?
11. What does board diversity mean to you, and what do you think a diverse board would look like at our organisation?
12. What do you consider to be the role of a non-executive director? How would you seek to clarify your role, if unclear?
13. How would you describe your style as a non-executive director?
14. What do you believe are the characteristics of an effective board?
15. What, in your view, is the leadership role of a non-executive?
16. How would you describe the ideal executive/non-executive relationship?
17. What would your relationship with our chair be like? How would you support and complement the Chair's role?

Commercial/business acumen

18. What relationships / contacts do you have with our key stakeholders?
19. How would you recommend we achieve our purpose and financial goals?
20. What could be further commercial opportunities for an organisation like ours?
21. What do you think of our structure and governance arrangements?
22. What does the current economic climate mean for us? What are the threats and opportunities?
23. Do you think you have the necessary experience to help

guide us through economic turbulence? Please give some relevant examples.
24. How do you feel your own background and experience could directly add value to our organisation?

The Organisation

25. What do you perceive are our current strategic considerations?
26. Are we doing enough to equip our members/ clients/ stakeholders for the challenges of the future?
27. Who do you consider to be our key stakeholders now and how may that change over the next 10-15 years?
28. What do you think our members/clients/stakeholders expect from us? How can we exceed these expectations?
29. What do you consider will be the key challenges facing our sector in the next 5-10 years?

Administrative

30. This role is not remunerated/unremunerated at $XXXXX. Could you confirm that you are comfortable with this?
31. How many other directorships do you have? Could you confirm that you are able to commit to the time required to perform effectively as a board member?
32. Is there anything that could potentially delay your availability to join our board?
33. Do you have any concerns about joining this board?
34. Are you aware of any potential conflicts of interest?

Closing questions

35. Is there anything we didn't ask you that you wanted to talk to us about?
36. Do you have any questions for us?

19 HOW LONG WILL IT TAKE TO BE APPOINTED?

A question I am often asked by members of Board Direction and non-members alike, is how long it will take to gain a board appointment. It's always difficult to provide a hard and fast answer to this question as there are always variables at play and everyone's journey will differ. However, as a rule - should you put your mind to it and follow the advice I provide - there is no reason that you cannot find yourself on a board (or a 'better' board) in the next 12 months - if not sooner.

However, for many that are searching for a board appointment perhaps the most difficult thing to do is to maintain the enthusiasm for the journey ahead. It is easy to become disgruntled. In fact, I spoke with a client recently who said just that - but after 6 months of searching, having his Board CV created, his LinkedIn profile updated and attending one of my masterclasses, he found his first Non-Executive Directorship - a Chair role of a prestigious Arts organisation. Which only goes to show that 'the harder you work the luckier you get'.

My board appointment journey

When I returned from my Executive Search career overseas I had only minor board experience and few relevant connections in Australia. I have long recognised the benefits of board appointments and wanted to contribute so it was my desire to find a new board appointment and I was able to do this within just 3 months of making the decision to do so. What counted in my favour was that I was clear about 3 things:

1. the sort of organisation that would value what I offered,
2. my skills and
3. the industry that I wanted to work in.

Being clear about these factors at the onset of my board search, and having a little luck, made my board journey a relatively short one.

Likewise, for you to have a successful and quick board appointment journey, you too should consider these 3 elements:

1. The sort of organisation that would value what you offer

Think about the scope and scale of your experience, to date - if you have worked for fairly small organisations, then aspiring to sit on a major board might be a misalignment. Equally, think about how much executive experience you have - if you have limited experience working with senior people or boards then this will also affect the sort of organisation that might appoint you to their board.

Finally, consider where your networks and connections lie - and more importantly, which sort of organisation is going to value them. Here you should pay particular attention to the organisations you have worked with in the past, their competitors or stakeholders, as this list can offer numerous opportunities for a hungry board candidate.

2. The skills you have to offer

Here think about what your core 'board' skills are. These will be similar to your executive experience but will need to be articulated differently. Remember that every board has a matrix of skills that they are looking to maintain. To be appointed you need to know that your skills are valuable and required. For example, there is perhaps no room on a board for another marketing expert and knowing this early is important.

Of course, don't just think about your executive skills. Consider also the experience you have gained across different sectors or industries. In essence, you must be able to articulate your experience to date and the skills you have gained in such a way that not only are they relevant to the board but also separate you from your competitors.

3. The industry you want to work in

Finally, you should consider which sector or industry you want a board appointment in and where you are likely to get the most traction. If you have worked in the Not-for-Profit space all your life but have an aspiration to sit on a retail board, you need to spend lots of time understanding what value you would offer to that industry - beyond just thinking that you can contribute. Aligning your aspirations with the realities is an important, though sometimes painful, process. Fortunately, one can swiftly move yourself from 'unappointable' to 'appointed'.

By keeping this in mind and applying it when you start your journey to being appointed to a board, you should well be able to **'dare them not to appoint you'**.

20 HOW MUCH CAN I EXPECT TO BE PAID?

A question that will undoubtedly come to mind as you start your journey to becoming a Board Member, is the question of how much you can expect to be paid as a member of a board.

The amount a Non-Executive could earn depends on a number of different factors. The most obvious are:

- The type of role you are appointed to;
- The sector the organisation operates in;
- The type of organisation;
- The size of the organisation;
- The turnover of the organisation.

Recent remuneration findings

Boards remunerate their members in several different ways - including daily sitting fees, annual fees, expenses, equity and additional committee fees. As such, board remuneration studies can struggle to gather enough information to be accurate and they often use relatively small sample sizes - further compounding any inaccuracies. Still it is possible to gather a strong sense of what you could expect to be paid if appointed to a board that remunerates.

The following remuneration reviews looked at different payment structures for Board Members:

Chair, Non-Executive and Committee member remuneration & allowances

Chair Remuneration

Study 1. A recent Australian study conducted found that Chairs were paid between $48k (medium unlisted) and $315k (ASX 200) with the average Chair remuneration being $139k.

Study 2. A more recent study - and, I think, an arguably better one, found that some chairs (of top percentile organisations by revenue) earned well over $600k and as little as $26. Looking at the remuneration, when considering the number of employees, found Chairs earn well over $700k and as little as $30k.

Non-Executive Remuneration

Study 1. Once again, using the data from the first study, we find that Non-Executive Directors are paid between $23k (small unlisted) and $137k (ASX200) with the average being $61k.

Study 2. Using the alternative broader study again we find, based on the industry of an organisation (rather than its size) we observe quite wide differences in what Non-Executive Directors are paid – from as little as $3k for health care providers up to over $327k for Banking boards.

Based on the revenue of a company and the number of employees, here the lower remuneration fees are $9k (Revenue $51k - $99k) and $7k (<250 employees) and up to $273k (Revenue

$1.5m+) and $323k (10,000+ employees).

Committee Remuneration

When we look at Committee Remuneration, we found that somewhere in the region of 30%-40% of organisations pay additional fees to their board members for taking on committee responsibilities.

Considering the historical amounts that Committee Members (both Chair and regular committee members) are paid for some of the most common committees that you might sit on, we found that an Audit Committee Chair roughly earns twice that of a regular Audit Committee member - $38k and $19k respectively.

Allowances

In addition to Committee-, Non-Executive- or Chair remuneration, 21% of directors also received a professional development allowance. The average amount being $3,786 per director.

The Pros and Cons of Not-for-Profit Board Member Remuneration

From the outset, it should probably be stated that organisations which operate in the 'Not-for-Profit (NfP)' or 'third sector' are incredibly diverse both in terms of the scope and scale of their operations. Whilst many NfPs confine their services to local communities and causes many others operate nationally or internationally and manage millions of dollars in operating budgets. To govern these sorts of organisations, the vast majority have recruited 'significant' board members who are passionate about the organisation's work and their own contribution.

My perspective

As an ex-board recruiter and passionate and unpaid not for profit board member myself let me nail my colours to the mast. I am in favour of remunerating all board members. Having said that, I do understand the difficulty that most NfPs face in doing this. However, from a recruiting perspective I, and my colleagues, have found it far easier to attract and retain quality candidates if a sitting fee is offered, even if it's fairly minor.

The statistics

As an overarching statement, it is fair to say I think that it is quite unusual for Not-for-Profits outside of large, complex entities such as health care systems or large foundations to remunerate their board members. In fact, a recent study suggested only 2% of Not-for-Profit Boards compensate their members. Another study suggested that 96% of Not-for-Profits have voluntary boards.

However, whilst few pay their members, most NfPs will offer to pay your expenses – although in reality I find few sitting board members claim these expenses, with the exception of major financial outlays.

Why don't they remunerate?

Generally, the argument is that board member compensation can call into question a non-profit's financial integrity and there is the belief that there should be no problem finding community leaders to serve as volunteer board members. Others believe that offering compensation might hinder a Not-for-Profit organisation's ability to recruit such board members.

To remunerate or not: three industry leaders weigh in

Three leaders in the Not-for-Profit sector weighed in on the matter of Not-for-Profit board member remuneration. This is what each of them had to say:

Member 1:

Generally speaking, I have no problem with Not-for-Profit (NFP) Non-Executive Directors being paid either by way of a director's fee or an honorarium. Instead of a blanket assumption of board volunteerism, the decision to pay or not to pay directors should be a matter entirely for each organisation. Respecting the autonomy of NFPs means accepting each NFP is the body best placed to decide whether paying non-executive directors fits within its organisational mission and values.

In seeking to move from a voluntary board to paid directors, NFPs should make a fully-informed decision that takes into account all legal implications, any funding limitations, disclosure arrangements and how the internal and external politics will play out.

Consideration of the politics surrounding remuneration is particularly important, given that the internal democratic processes of many NFPs may be disturbed by changing the voluntary nature of the board and by external reaction from funders, major donors or the general public. All in all, I would counsel to hasten slowly towards any move to remunerate.

Member 2:

NFPs are tackling some of the most important issues that our community is facing; so why do we expect a bunch of volunteers to maintain the helm of the board? In addition, most NFPs have tax concessions. As they are managing taxpayer-funded resources, they need directors of the highest calibre.

Many of us have seen the "star-studded" NFP board; the board with an array of talented board members, over-achievers, who individually have had successful corporate careers and have brilliant resumes. Unfortunately, this often means that they are in demand and have insufficient time available for their NFP position. They are trying to find time to fulfil their NFP board responsibilities among many competing priorities such as their paid employment, family and social commitments. The danger is that the NFP receives the lowest priority as it is for "unpaid service", compared to paid employment or paid board positions. Their conscience is appeased by the knowledge that they are not receiving remuneration for their effort. Of course, this is fraught with danger as legally they have similar responsibilities as for-profit boards.

Being on a NFP board is often more difficult than a for-profit board. You are likely to be tackling significant social issues with limited resources and few options to raise capital, and where outcomes measurement is difficult. With payment should come greater commitment to professionalise NFP boards, greater focus on outcomes and measurement of board performance. Payment would provide a stronger sense of contract. Shouldn't we demand the best board members for our NFPs? And pay them appropriately?

Of course, many NFPs do not have the balance sheet to support paying board members. If you can't afford to pay for board members, or find funding partners to assist, then clearly it would be foolish to do so. A step in the right direction would be arming our NFP boards with the best talent in the country and paying them appropriately.

Member 3:
The suggestion to directors of charities that they be remunerated, would I think be greeted by the vast majority with a

mixture of puzzlement and offence. Why? Because they give their time to provide the governance function of the organisation as committed supporters of the cause. The idea of these directors being paid runs directly contrary to their intention to contribute to the purpose of the charity.

So why is the question even being raised? Two reasons. First, charities have moved way beyond "volunteerism" in the unfortunately pejorative sense of being run by unpaid, part-time amateurs rather than highly professional and competent paid employees. And some are also questioning the assumption that the governance function should be provided by unpaid volunteers, albeit they are for the most part highly experienced and professional directors.

Second, in some specific parts of the charity sector it is becoming increasingly difficult to find the kind of committed directors who have the skills, experience and time necessary to govern the larger, more complex and highly regulated enterprises that charities have become.

Directors are not always unpaid. Payment of directors has been the practice in a few specific kinds of charities – in health, for example. However, in my experience this is still not at all the norm in Australia. Payment is not expected where there is an active community of interest and commitment that makes up the supporter base and to whom the directors are accountable. It is probably more easily justifiable by directors where they are self-appointing and they are not accountable to a larger member or supporter base. This is the case particularly where the income of the organisation comes predominantly from grants and government funding rather than supporter donations.

This is not at all to imply any criticism of directors who do decide to remunerate themselves, because it is essential that boards attract the right talent. After all, we do not have the same sensitivity about remuneration of employees, provided that it is not excessive. Payment of directors may attract a wider range of skills, age and socio-economic profile, which would be a positive outcome. While this is desirable, I am still ambivalent. I can't help thinking something will be irrecoverably lost.

Remuneration makes no difference

Those in favour of NfP board member remuneration argue that it can help improve board diversity, attract highly skilled professionals and those who cannot afford to take the role unpaid.

While this is also my view, there are nonetheless some studies that suggest that there is little evidence paying Not-for-Profit Board Members improves recruitment or retention. A recent study of US non-profit organisations found no indication that compensating these sort of board members promoted higher levels of board engagement, encouraged greater board diversity or attracted candidates with specialist expertise.

With most registered charities having low revenues, most cannot afford to pay their board members anyway.

Conclusion

Developing a portfolio career can be lucrative. However, for many the opportunity to serve on a board for an organisation that they are passionate about is all the reward required. Regardless of your motivation board work is incredibly rewarding but requires dedication and passion. To achieve your board aspirations, you need access to board opportunities and know how to **'dare them not to appoint you'**.

21 YOU HAVE BEEN OFFERED A POSITION

Congratulations! All the research and energy you put into your application and the subsequent interview paid off - you have been offered a position on the board.

STEPS TO ACCEPTING

What next?
Whilst immediately accepting an appointment can be very tempting, many experienced NED's first response to this kind of offer is 'No'. Their response is such because the reputational, financial and social risks involved in sitting on a board are considerable. For this reason, you should critically assess several aspects prior to agreeing to take on a board position.

Letter of appointment
Above all else, you should ask to see a draft letter of appointment and the organization's Constitution and/or Board Charter.

Make sure that you also find out about:

1. The **terms and conditions** (including the term) of appointment.

2. The **remuneration** (if any).

3. How **expenses** are reimbursed.

4. What **director's insurance cover** there is.

5. Whether there is an **induction program** for new directors.

6. What **continuing education** is expected or provided.

7. The nature of board and director **evaluation**.

8. **Director-related policies**, such as share trading guidelines (where relevant) or ability to seek legal advice at company expense.

The points above provide only a basis for further investigation. You should now undertake a full due diligence review.

Due diligence

The range of information that you may need to make an informed decision when considering a position will vary according to your personal circumstances and what the organisation does. However, there are three key sources of information that you may choose to use to do your due diligence:

- Publicly available information
- The organization's staff and stakeholders

- Your own personal networks.

Publicly available information

This is usually found in company reports or on their website. Using these resources is an obvious place to begin. Expand on the research you did before your interview. It should be easy to understand quickly from looking at the organization's website or annual report - what it does, how it makes money (if it is a not-for-profit, what is its goal or focus?) and what are its key strengths. If it isn't, what does this say about the organisation and your role on the board?

Don't forget to do an Internet search on the organisation and read relevant business / industry / sector articles. Don't necessarily be put off by what you find, rather treat it as being forewarned and forearmed. Instead, consider how the board responds to the issues and criticisms.

You should also ask to see the last 6 months of board papers. These should be read thoroughly and questions posed to the Chairman based on your observations of this and the board meeting.

You may be familiar with the organisation but it is still worth taking a step back and trying to judge how external stakeholders see it. You can get all sorts of information about the organisation from public sources, but this provides little insight into the people you may be working with.

Staff and stakeholders

Upon being asked to join the board you should request to sit in on a board meeting. This can give you an insight into the dynamics of the board.

You should also ask to speak with the CEO and CFO (separately) and any other key senior executives. This is a, confidential, opportunity to ask the questions that you perhaps could not ask at board level. It is a good opportunity to ask questions around how the board approaches risk. After all, they may be your risks to consider soon and you will be responsible, and held accountable, for the actions of the organisation.

Ask when the board was last evaluated and whether you can see the results (confidentially). If it has not been reviewed, ask why not. If the response given is because they are performing well or there is no need, you may want to consider the motivations for this -arrogance or fear are two possible motivations. Both you should be aware of.

If you have not already, research who are the key stakeholders for this organisation. Are there local communities who depend on the organisation? Is it an organisation that is (or could become) in the public eye?

Personal connections

Speak with your personal networks to find out as much as you can about the organisation/board. In most cases, they will have something to say that is constructive. If you have existing connections with stakeholders who have an interest in the organisation arrange to have a meeting. It is good networking but can also be very informative on how the organisation is viewed in the sector.

Finally, consider whether your existing relationships might be impacted upon on becoming a director in this new organisation. It could mean a fundamental change to existing relationships because of a perceived conflict of interest.

You may also wish to consider a number of specific board-related aspects including reviewing:

The financials

Understanding the financial situation of the organisation is arguably the most important aspect contributing to your decision as to whether to join the board or not.

One of the best ways to understand the finances of the organisation is to speak to the Auditors. As mentioned earlier, arranging to speak with the CEO and /or CFO separately is also highly recommended.

The Board and Executive

Do not assume that because there are well-known 'names' on the board, that it is a functional board or a well-governed organisation. There are several high-profile organizations that have had high profile boards where significant governance issues have arisen. Remember that any board can operate well in the good times.

The real test of the strength of a board is when things get difficult and relationships are stretched. You may want to think carefully about joining a board where the CEO and chairman are close personal friends (or the same person), or the majority of the directors are personal friends. These close relationships are highly likely to have some impact on the board dynamics and your effectiveness.

Your role

How hands-on will your role be? Will you be expected to get involved in the detail and do hands-on work, or sit on a large number of subcommittees?

If you are replacing a retiring director, consider in what sort of role they were placed in the organisation. If it is a direct - like for like - replacement, it would be safe to assume that you might carry the same sort of commitments they did.

Beyond the board meetings themselves, many organizations want more from their NEDs. For example, many not for profits expect you to help fundraise (or even financially contribute) to the running of the organisation. This may mean using your personal connections to raise the profile of the organisation or raise donations. How comfortable are you in doing this?

The cultural 'fit'

When it comes to assessing your 'fit' for a particular board, you might first consider how you will be able to make a valuable contribution. Based on your prior research, what you know about the board members, what you have seen of their actions (and reactions), think about how you will be able contribute positively to the future of the organisation.

Passion

Finally, ask yourself, after all your deliberations, whether you are passionate about serving as part this board. Paid or unpaid, serving on a board can seem overly time-consuming and when you do the math, poorly paid.

When this feels particularly the case, what will often keep you going is that you are enjoying yourself and feel like you are making a difference. The key to ensure that you feel this way, is the right mix of board members, support, an honest belief in what the organisation does and that you can contribute. If these elements are not in play, then many just don't see serving on a board worth the risk or investment of their time and energy.

22 BOARD APPOINTMENT RESOURCES

Board Vacancy Websites

www.boarddirection.com.au - the most comprehensive and diverse list of board vacancies in Australia.

www.probono.com.au - an advertiser of primarily voluntary executive and board vacancies.

www.ourcommunity.com.au - another advertiser of primarily unpaid executive and board vacancies.

Board Advertisements

- LinkedIn
- MyCareer
- Seek
- National/State Newspapers

- Trade Magazines

Recruiters (the ones I like)

- Board Advice (WA)
- Boomerang Consulting (NSW)
- Dakin Mayers (VIC)
- Derwent Executive (NSW)
- Directors Australia (QLD)
- SACS (VIC)
- Slade Partners (VIC)
- Talent 2 (National)
- Third Sector People (NSW)
- Watermark (NSW)

Governance Training

- The Governance Institute of Australia
www.governanceinstitute.com.au

- The Australian Institute of Company Directors
www.companydirectors.com.au

23 INTRODUCING THE NON-EXECUTIVE DIRECTOR PROGRAM

Do you know why most people who want to become a non-executive director don't achieve their board aspirations despite their desire to do so?

A highly competitive process

Be under no illusion, gaining a board appointment is a highly competitive process with far more candidates than there are opportunities. For most of you, you will already know this to be the case as:

- you have probably been considering gaining a board appointment for some time but don't quite know where to begin or
- you already have a board appointment but are struggling to find you next one or
- you already have a successful career but want to complement it with a board directorship and are struggling to find the time to search for opportunities successfully or
- you just can't find the knowledge you need to turn your aspirations into reality.

For these reasons, I developed the Non-Executive Program. It provides the practical help required to gain your first or a subsequent board appointment – no matter what your aspirations are or where you are in your career.

Introducing the Non-Executive Program

I want to introduce you to the Non-Executive Program - the best program of its kind (and perhaps the only one) in the world. It is something that I have personally developed utilising over a decade of board recruitment experience, having reviewed over 10,000 board applications and interviewed thousands of board candidates as well as working with hundreds of Chairs recruiting new non-executive directors for them. In short, this experience has led to the development of a 12-month course that explicitly sets out before you the foundations, the steps and the templates you need to gain a board appointment.

It is utterly unique and the best way for you to achieve your board aspirations – no matter what they are – and get appointed. It cost many thousands of dollars to develop and over four years of my life. It incorporates not just my knowledge as an international board recruiter; it also stems from the combined knowledge of the thousands of candidates I have interviewed and the hundreds of Chairs I have worked with in my capacity as an International headhunter/recruiter. Thus, I believe that we have developed the most effective, the most practical and the most valuable course of its type in the world. There is genuinely nothing else like it.

Do we guarantee to get you a board appointment? We can't – no one can because no one can interview on your behalf. However, and for that reason, within the Non-Executive Program we include a Board Interview Training service – a service that prepares you fully for a non-executive interview and will drastically alter the way you perform in an interview.

Reviews & Success

Does what we offer work? You bet. Board Direction has worked with over 1,500 clients and over 40,000 receive our weekly board search advice newsletters and board vacancy alerts. We could not have gained or maintained this level of support if what we did, didn't work.

There are hundreds of examples of the success we have offered others and could offer you. However, one client with our help was almost immediately appointed to a board because of the Board CV we wrote and the advice we provided for him:

'Why do I know the Board CV was a catalyst? Because I asked what attracted their attention to me, to which they responded "the style, format and clearly articulated content of the CV". Thank you for assisting me to make this first step into directorship outside of my own company and good luck to you in continuing your worthy business.'

Thousands of others have attended our Board Search Masterclasses and Board Search Breakfasts – typical scores are 9/10 with reviews such as this one:

'Wow! I have received valuable information that will allow me to achieve more success in my pursuit of my next board position. 10/10.' Robert 2015

We are so confident in the Non-Executive Program that if, having completed the course, you don't think the services we offer were of value, we will give you 100% of your money back.

Included in the Non-Executive Program

Remember, the Non-Executive Program has been developed for those who want to ensure that they are best placed for a board appointment - it is a full 12-month program. It is absolutely our best work and has been developed utilising over a decade of practical experience of putting people on boards - it is only course of its type in the world. So here is what I am giving you:

- ✓ **Board Vacancies:** Immediate and 2 years of access to thousands of board vacancies.
- ✓ **A bespoke Board CV written for you:** By David Schwarz: Australia's leading board appointment professional.
- ✓ **LinkedIn Profile Writing:** Utilising your new Board CV as a basis, we will craft or create a LinkedIn profile that evidences your ability to successfully reach your board aspirations.
- ✓ **LinkedIn Training:** By David Schwarz – A Top 10 LinkedIn user with over 23,000 connections. Understanding how to leverage LinkedIn as a cornerstone to gaining board positions.
- ✓ **Interview Preparation:** A real interview with a real recruiter with the honest feedback you won't get from anyone else.
- ✓ **Application Writing:** We will write your first application for you – the basis of which we will use for future applications.

- ✓ **Application Critiquing:** No matter how many boards you apply for, we will critique and edit every application before submission.
- ✓ **The Board Search Course:** A 12-month course covering, among others, the following topics:
  - *Introduction to how you find a board appointment;*
  - *What Chairs look for in new board members – the five essential & other desirable criteria & governance training;*
  - *What sort of board role is right for you;*
  - *How to define your own board profile – addressing the five key areas;*
  - *The value of proper research & how it can separate you from others;*
  - *How board members are appointed;*
  - *How to write a 'board ready' resume – one that works;*
  - *How to write a non-executive application & cover letter;*
  - *Non-Executive Interviews – What you are likely to be asked and how to respond;*
  - *Post a successful or unsuccessful application – what to do next.*
- ✓ **Monthly Coaching Sessions:** It is easy to lose the motivation to keep chasing board opportunities. Our monthly coaching and support will hold you accountable and ensure your long-term success.
- ✓ **Board Search Masterclass (in person):** Run in Sydney, Melbourne & Brisbane twice a year. Meet David Schwarz – Australia's leading board recruitment expert - and you will find out how to *dare them not to appoint you.*
- ✓ **Board Search E-Masterclass (online):** A 10-part video series of the live Board Search Masterclass led by David Schwarz – Australia's leading board recruitment expert. Viewable immediately and at your leisure, you will find out how to *dare them not to appoint you.*
- ✓ **NED Introductions:** We will introduce you to, and set up meetings with, up to 10 active Australian Non-Executive

Directors – relevant but outside of your usual network - to help you build relationships that count.
- ✓ **Weekly Board Appointment Advice:** Emailed to you each week and providing the insider knowledge you need to stay focused and gain an appointment.
- ✓ **25% Off:** All additional Board Direction products and services.

No one is more experienced than we are in helping people fast track a board appointment; Board Direction has helped more people than anyone else to gain a seat at the board table. This absolutely is the best program for non-executives we could think of.

Is the Non-Executive Program for You?

This is <u>not</u> a governance course. We pick up where governance courses leave off. This is a course to help you gain a board appointment. As such, we begin in the belief that you are either interested in gaining a board directorship and/or are qualified do so. (If you would like to undertake some formal governance training you should contact the Governance Institute of Australia).

The Non-Executive Program was developed for individuals who are determined to gain a board appointment and are willing to push themselves to achieve their board aspirations. For some, finding time to pursue their ambitions, will be difficult; which is why this Program incorporates monthly personal accountability catchups. For others, the challenge might be underestimating or not realizing how valuable their skills are, so we work closely with you to articulate your value at board level and then find appropriate opportunities for you.

You might have used similar career services in the past with over-priced consultants providing poor value. You might feel like you did not get any value from it. For this reason, we clearly list each of the services we will provide and their associated timings.

We will do all we can to tailor this Program to your needs but it still might be that the program is not right for you. The timing might not be right, you might not have the money or you don't want to commit the time. If this is the case, you should look at the ACCESS, ACCESS+ or EXECUTIVE membership options, which still provide access to the board vacancies, a board CV and the Masterclass but are cheaper and require less intensity. You can find more information on these by visiting our website: https://boarddirection.com.au/membership/

Why don't most people achieve their board aspirations?

It is simple – more often than not, they don't understand the nuances of the board appointment process and don't persevere where others might. Don't let that be you - the Non-Executive Program is the best way to ensure you will gain a board appointment.

Statistics have shown that people that have Board Directorships in addition to an executive role are more appointable, earn more, are unemployed less and have better networks and connections. They are also able to future-proof their careers better, have more successful retirements and weather career change better. Still, not everyone is suited to a board appointment. Equally, the Non-Executive Program is not suitable for everyone as not everyone can afford the time required to dedicate themselves to achieving their aspirations.

But, if you do have the desire to get onto a board, to drive your career forward with a board appointment, to transition from full-time work to a portfolio of part-time board directorships or to develop a portfolio career, then the Non-Executive Program is for you – it is the best out there and there is nothing else like it.

Visit the Board Direction website at www.boarddirection.com.au to sign up and dare them not to appoint you.

Money Back Guarantee

We are so confident in the Non-Executive Program that if, after completing the program, you don't think the services we offered was of value to you, we will give 100% of your money back – guaranteed.

24 HOW CAN BOARD DIRECTION HELP?

- **Board Vacancies**

Access to Australia's largest and most diverse list of non-executive board vacancies across the Commercial (ASX, SME, Large), Public (Government Boards & Committees) and Not-for-Profit (the big ones and small ones) sectors.

- **Board CV Writing**

A Board Ready CV is different in terms of tone, content and structure and can make the difference between a success application and an unsuccessful one. So, regardless of how much weight you think a board resume carries (they carry a lot of weight) it is best to get one professionally written at the beginning of your board search.

- **LinkedIn Profile Writing**

As a Top 10 Australian LinkedIn user with over 23,000 LinkedIn connections and having written hundreds of Board CV's, there are few more qualified to update/write your new LinkedIn profile for you.

- **Profile on the NED Directory**

Think of it as a LinkedIn for NED's. This unique service offers the opportunity for you to be recruited by hundreds of organizations each year that are looking for new board members.

- **Board Search E-Course**

Access all the knowledge and information you need to gain a board appointment. This course was written and presented by David Schwarz, Australia's leading board recruitment expert and author of *The Board Appointments Book - How to gain a Non-Executive Directorship*.

The E-Course contains a suite of 10 separate training units that take you through, in detail, the practicalities of gaining a board appointment, including:

- How to find the right board for you – how to target the most appropriate opportunities.
- Understanding what Chairs want in a successful board candidate – how to address their five core criteria.
- How to write your Board Profile – one that articulates why you should be appointed.
- How to get a Board Appointment – the research you need to do and understanding the importance of the Chair.
- How to Develop Personal Connections and The Direct Approach – developing strong and weak ties and using LinkedIn effectively.
- How to work successfully with Executive Search Firms and respond to advertisements – understanding their role and the importance of reputation.
- How to write Supporting Statements & Cover Letters –

templates and practical responses are provided.
- How to write a compelling Board CV/Resume – template provided with detailed discussion.
- How to deliver a successful Non-Executive Interview – over 30 board questions provided and how to answer them.
- How to determine whether an offer is right for you – the due diligence you should do and how to leverage your appointment.

In addition to the units above, the course concludes with the full access to the ten-part Board Appointments Masterclass. Here you can watch David Schwarz present, live, the Masterclass.

The course also contains practical anecdotes from recruiters and Chairs that highlight what is required to be appointed to a board and provide insights into the murky world of board recruitment.

Each unit is supported with a dedicated task, template or further reading that will prompt you to go to the lengths you need to be appointed.

By completing this course, you will not only have the knowledge of how to position yourself appropriately to gain any board appointment but also have the practical knowledge and templates to be able to do this swiftly and professionally. The result being that you will be more prepared than any other candidates and will truly be able to *dare them not to appoint you*.

- **Board Search Masterclass**

Gaining a Non-Executive Board Directorship is a competitive process. This Masterclass provides all the practical skills, templates and knowledge you need to get the board appointment that you want. Designed specifically for people who are motivated to 'shortcut' their journey to obtaining their first, subsequent or bigger board position. This class is not for everyone. Some find the advice daunting whilst others thrive in gaining practical advice and guidance in how to get the board role that they have always wanted. So, if you are serious about getting started or developing a portfolio career then this is the course for you. Presented by David Schwarz – Australia's leading board recruitment expert.

- **Board Search E-Masterclass**

In more detail than you will find anywhere else, hear David Schwarz – Australia's leading board recruitment expert - address practical steps you need to take to get your first or next board appointment.

Specifically, each masterclass will address the following elements:

- What board is right for you – how to set your expectations to avoid disappointment.
- What boards look for in new board members – five key areas.
- How to define your own board profile – addressing the five key areas.
- How 70% of board members were appointed to their current board – and how to do it yourself using your personal connections.
- How to use recruiters to get appointed – who to use, where to find them and how to work with them effectively.
- How to respond to advertisements – what really counts and what doesn't.
- How to get your current resume and cover letter 'board ready' – with practical templates.

- What you are likely to be asked in a board interview – and how to respond.

In addition, you will receive board CV templates, cover letter templates and gain access to countless insights from both recruiters and Chairs involved in board recruitment.

- **Application Review**

Board applications differ from regular executive applications in terms of the tone, content and style. Not having bespoke documents that meet the criteria set out - an appropriate cover letter or board CV - will all limit your chances of being selected for an interview or be appointed. Don't let a poor application that doesn't address the five key criteria that all Chairs and recruiters look for, negatively impact your application.

Before you submit an application for any non-executive directorship let David Schwarz – Australia's leading board recruitment expert with over a decade of experience of putting people on boards – review and critique your application documents to improve your chances of success.

The number of applications reviewed within 12 months is unlimited. So, no matter how many applications you decide to submit, we will be with you each time to help you refine your messaging and prompting you to do more to ensure that you separate yourself from your competitors.

- **Personal Monthly Coaching & Accountability Sessions**

Gaining a good board appointment takes time and is challenging at the best of times but the rewards are significant for those who persevere. However, if your messaging is wrong, if you don't understand how board appointments work and how to subvert these 'rules', then your perseverance alone might not be enough.

This service will ensure that your journey towards gaining your first or a subsequent board appointment is successful. E-monthly coaching and accountability session with David Schwarz – Australia's leading board recruitment expert who has over a decade of experience putting people on boards – will ensure that the time you spend gets traction and results in opportunities that you might have otherwise thought were impossible. He will hold you to account to both your board aspirations and the work you need to undertake to achieve them.

Specifically, you will receive:

1. Monthly personal & bespoke 1:1 coaching and accountability sessions (via Skype, in person or by phone) with David Schwarz.
2. Plus, over 12 months you will complete the E- Board Search Course (containing a suite of 10 separate training units that take you through, in detail, the practicalities of gaining a board appointment. You can view more details regarding the E-Board Search Course above.

- **LinkedIn Training**

LinkedIn should be the cornerstone of your board search efforts. We will teach you how to create new relationships that lead to board positions.

All training sessions are led by David Schwarz – a top 10 LinkedIn user with over 23,000 connections. He is Australia's leading board recruitment expert and will teach you how to use LinkedIn effectively and how to leverage it powerfully to gain a board appointment.

- **Personal Application Writing**

A fully comprehensive board application writing service where we will craft your full board application – CV, Supporting Statement & Cover Letter.

With this service you have two options, one with and the other without a Board CV.

Personal Application Writing – NOT including Board CV

If you HAVE a board CV already then this is the product for you.

Board applications differ from regular executive applications in terms of tone, content and style. Not having bespoke documents that meet the criteria set out, will impact and drastically limit your chances of being selected for an interview or be appointed.

David Schwarz has over a decade of experience putting people on boards as an ex-board recruiter. He has written conservatively 1,500 board CVs in his time and reviewed thousands. Working closely with you, he will personally write your board application per the specifications required by the advertising organisation.

Typically, this service will include:

- Personal conversations to understand your drivers and successes
- A bespoke board cover letter written for you
- A bespoke supporting statement addressing the core criteria written for you

Personal Application Writing – including Board CV

If you DON'T HAVE a board CV, then this is the product for you.

Typically, this service will include:

- Personal conversations to understand your drivers and successes
- A bespoke board CV written for you
- A bespoke board cover letter written for you
- A bespoke supporting statement addressing the core criteria written for you

However, with both these services, David won't leave you there. He will further critique and amend the application until you are content that it accurately reflects the message you would like to portray.

Don't let a poor application that doesn't address the five key criteria that all Chairs and recruiters look for negatively impact your application.

• Personal Career Planning Session

Define your board career aspirations and the plan the journey towards achieving them with David Schwarz – Australia's leading board recruitment expert.

Gaining a good board appointment takes time and is challenging at the best of times but the rewards are significant for those who persevere. *The harder you work the luckier you get* is a common phrase and one that many try to apply when searching for a board appointment. Unfortunately, if your messaging is wrong, if you don't understand how board appointments work and how to subvert the 'rules', then you could be wasting your time.

An intensive Board Career Planning session with David Schwarz will ensure that the time you spend gets traction and results in opportunities that you might otherwise have thought were impossible.

In your Planning Session, we will comprehensively:

- Define your board career aspirations
- Define appropriate board possibilities
- Articulate your Board Profile – your pitch
- Review your current CV – making it more board appropriate
- Create a list of individual connections to network with

This is both an educational service and a practical one. So, in reality, this service spans two separate sessions. The first, either in person, Skype or by phone, we cover the items above. The second, by phone or Skype, we follow up on the actions agreed upon and to further develop your forward plan.

This Board Career Planning session is designed to help you achieve your board goals.

• Mock Board Interview / Interview Training

Board interviews differ from executive interviews in terms of the content, style and approach. Further, not understanding what boards want to hear from applicants or how to articulate your response to the questions they ask, will ultimately result in an unsuccessful process.

This service offers a full 2-hour mock board interview scenario with David Schwarz – Australia's leading board recruitment expert and ex board head hunter who has interviewed thousands – and critical feedback. This is guaranteed to give you the language confidence you need to *dare them not to appoint you*.

You will also receive a subsequent phone call prior to the interview to reinforce the lessons learnt and to prepare you fully for a successful interview.

- **Personal NED introductions**

65% of board appointments occur via a personal connection – you need to get introduced to the right people.

Are you relying on stale or outdated personal connections to try to find a board appointment? We can introduce you to the people you need to know to successfully develop a board career or gain your first non-executive directorship.

With a database of 23,000+ non-executives and 20,000+ LinkedIn connections, Board Direction is highly connected. Utilising these connections, we will personally introduce you to Non-Executives in your chosen and related fields. These relationships, in addition to our personal recommendation, will fuel your board aspirations and result in more opportunities with organizations that you might not usually have access to.

Specifically, you will receive:

- personal introductions to up to 20 non-executive directors
- bespoke board profile development
- an intensive one on one board career development session with David Schwarz
- a bespoke LinkedIn tutorial
- LinkedIn Profile update.

- **Non-Executive Director Program**

The Non-Executive Director Program has been developed for those who want to ensure that they are best placed for a board appointment - it is a full 12-month program. It is absolutely our best work and has been developed utilising over a decade of practical experience of putting people on boards - it is the only course of its type in the world. You can read more about it in the previous chapter.

For more information please visit
www.boarddirection.com.au

25 FINAL THOUGHTS

Finding a board position is not a simple or quick process, nor should it be. Not everyone is suited to being a Board Director - the role requires a special combination of skills and experience. Be honest in your assessment of your strengths and weaknesses before starting the journey. There may be other, more appropriate and rewarding, avenues for you to become involved with, or contribute to an organisation you are interested in. Ask yourself honestly, *'Am I the right person for this organisation or for board work in general?'*

A board directorship can be one of the most rewarding experiences you will have in your professional life. However, to make a success of it you should start early. Finding your first or a subsequent appointment is a time-consuming process and having counseled numerous clients - ex CEOs and retired Directors in particular - who say that they want to sit on a board <u>now</u> but do not have any board experience - the reality is they should have started their search and board career long ago for their ambitions to become a reality.

Be prepared for the application and search process to be more thorough and lengthier than you may ordinarily be used to.

Further, by: taking the time to thoroughly prepare yourself; by doing thorough research that incorporates developing new personal connections and; by conducting proper due diligence on the organisation will make your journey more enjoyable and improve your chances of success.

And, of course, don't forget that the best non-executive directors never stop learning and are passionate about what they do. Continuing your professional development is critical to maximizing your chances of being a successful director and making a valuable contribution to board and organizational performance. Equally, learning from other directors will be key to your success.

It is a terrific journey - start now, good luck and don't forget to **'dare them not to appoint you'**.

David Schwarz

Practical Advice for Finding and Gaining
a
Non-Executive Directorship

www.boarddirection.com.au

ABOUT THE AUTHOR

There are few more qualified to explain the non-executive recruitment process, and how to gain a board appointment than David Schwarz. He is the MD of Board Direction (www.boarddirection.com.au) - an organisation dedicated to putting people on boards. With over a decade of experience as both an international headhunter and non-executive recruiter, he has interviewed well over a thousand board members and has been quoted as a 'CV expert' by mainstream media. He is also a Top 10 LinkedIn user with over 23,000 connections. He is a regular speaker on the board appointments process and is himself a non-executive director. For these reasons, he brings the in-depth and practical experience that few possess.

Printed in Great Britain
by Amazon